TWAYNE'S MASTERWORK STUDIES
Robert Lecker, General Editor

Sons AND *Lovers*
A NOVEL OF
DIVISION AND DESIRE

Ross C Murfin

TWAYNE PUBLISHERS • BOSTON
A Division of G. K. Hall & Co.

Sons and Lovers: A Novel of Division and Desire
Ross C Murfin

Twayne's Masterwork Studies No. 7

Copyright 1987 by G. K. Hall & Co.
All rights reserved.
Published by Twayne Publishers
A Division of G. K. Hall & Co.
70 Lincoln Street
Boston, Massachusetts 02111

Passages from *Sons and Lovers* by
D. H. Lawrence copyright 1964,
1971 by Angelo Ravagli and
C. M. Weekley, executors of
The Estate of Freida Lawrence
Ravagli. Reprinted by
permission of Viking Penguin Inc.

Copyediting supervised by Lewis DeSimone
Book production by Janet Zietowski

Typeset in 10/14 Sabon
by Compset, Inc.

Printed on permanent/durable acid-free paper
and bound in the United States of America

Library of Congress Cataloging in Publication Data

Murfin, Ross C.
Sons and lovers.

(Twayne's masterwork studies; no. 7)
Bibliography: p.
Includes index.
1. Lawrence, David Herbert, 1885–1930. Sons and
    lovers. I. Title. II. Series.
PR6023.A93S6835   1987   823'.912   87-8612
ISBN 0-8057-7967-1
ISBN 0-8057-8007-6 (pbk. : alk. paper)

CONTENTS

NOTE ON REFERENCES
AND ACKNOWLEDGMENTS

The first edition of *Sons and Lovers* was published by Duckworth and Son in 1913. In the same year, an American edition of the novel was printed by Mitchell Kennerly. *Sons and Lovers* was republished in the United States by the Viking Press in 1933, and since then it has appeared, both in the United States and in Great Britain, in numerous Viking, Viking Compass, Viking Penguin, and Penguin editions. In preparing this study of the novel, I have quoted from the readily available Penguin edition, which appeared in paperback in 1976 and has subsequently been reprinted eight times. It is worth noting, however, that most editions of the novel are almost identical, even in pagination; thus, virtually all references to the Penguin edition serve as accurate references to the Random House/Modern Library edition, which was first published in 1962 by arrangement with the Viking Press.

All citations of *Sons and Lovers* following the first have been made, in parentheses, within the body of my text. Quotations from works other than *Sons and Lovers* have been footnoted sequentially from the beginning to the end of this book; the Notes section is located after the last chapter.

The frontispiece portrait of D. H. Lawrence is a reproduction of a silverpoint drawing made by Patrick Donovan. Silverpoint is an ancient art form involving the use of a silver wire; it was popular during the Renaissance but is very seldom practiced today. Mr. Donovan is a law-enforcement officer in Somerville, New Jersey. He is a graduate of the University of Miami.

D. H. Lawrence
Portrait by Patrick Donovan, 1986.

CHRONOLOGY: D. H. LAWRENCE'S LIFE AND WORKS

1885	David Herbert Lawrence born 11 September in Eastwood, Nottinghamshire, to Arthur Lawrence and Lydia Beardsall Lawrence.
1898	Begins attending Nottingham High School on scholarship.
1901	Death of brother, William Ernest Lawrence (William in *Sons and Lovers*). Lawrence meets Jessie Chambers (Miriam) and goes to work for a firm manufacturing surgical appliances.
1902	Accepts position as (uncertified) teacher in Eastwood.
1905	Composes his earliest poems, "Guelder Roses" and "Campions."
1906	Enters teacher-training course offered at University College, Nottingham.
1907	Writing *The White Peacock*. Publishes story "A Prelude" in *Nottinghamshire Guardian*.
1908	Awarded teachers certificate by University College. Obtains teaching position, Davidson Road School, Croydon (South London).
1909	Jessie Chambers submits Lawrence's early poems to the *English Review*, which publishes them. Relationship develops between Lawrence and fellow schoolteacher Helen Corke.
1910	Begins writing *The Trespasser*. Becomes engaged to Louisa (Louie) Burrows. Lawrence's mother ill with cancer. Death of mother, 9 December.
1910	Working on a new novel, "Paul Morel" (later to become *Sons and Lovers*).
1911	*The White Peacock* published in January. In November, Lawrence falls ill with pneumonia, stops teaching.

1912   Resigns teaching position in February. In April, meets Frieda
               von Richthofen Weekley, wife of professor at University Col-
               lege, Nottingham, second daughter of Baron Friedrich von
               Richthofen, and distant cousin of Manfred von Richthofen,
               the flying ace better known as the "Red Baron." In May, elopes
               with Frieda to Germany and Italy. *The Trespasser* published.
               Writes poems about relationship with Frieda, revises *Sons and
               Lovers.*

1913   *Love Poems and Others* published in February, *Sons and Lov-
               ers* in May. Writing *Twilight in Italy*. Returns to England from
               the Continent, begins work on "The Sisters" (later *The Rain-
               bow* and *Women in Love*).

1914   Frieda granted a divorce, marries Lawrence in July. England
               goes to war against Germany (World War I). Lawrence takes
               a walking tour of the Lake District, works on "The Sisters"
               and *Study of Thomas Hardy*. *The Prussian Officer and Other
               Stories* published.

1915   *The Rainbow* published but suppressed by court order in No-
               vember. Lawrence and Frieda move to Cornwall, plan to travel
               to America, apply for passports. Lawrence working on
               Women in Love.

1916   *Twilight in Italy* and a volume of poems, *Amores*, published.
               Lawrence and Frieda continue living in Cornwall.

1917   Found medically unfit for military service. Writes "The Reality
               of Peace," begins work on *Studies in Classic American Liter-
               ature*. Publication of *Look! We Have Come Through!*, mostly
               written in 1912. Lawrence and Frieda denied passports, ex-
               pelled from Cornwall on suspicion of being German sympa-
               thizers, spies.

1918   Reexamined by army, again found unfit.

1919   Falls seriously ill with influenza. Finishes draft of *Aaron's Rod*.
               Lawrence and Frieda given permission to leave England.
               Frieda goes to Germany in October, Lawrence to Turin, then
               to Florence, Italy. Reunited, the two go to Capri.

1920   Living with Frieda in Capri, Florence, and Taormina, Sicily,
               Lawrence writes the first of the poems later to be published in
               Birds, Beasts and Flowers. In addition, works on *Aaron's Rod,
               The Lost Girl, Psychoanalysis and the Unconscious*, and a re-
               vised version of *Studies in Classic American Literature.*

1921   Visits Sardinia and writes *Sea and Sardinia*. Also working on
               Fantasia of the Unconscious. Finishes *Aaron's Rod*. *Psycho-
               analysis of the Unconscious* published.

Chronology

1922   *Aaron's Rod* published in the spring, *Fantasia of the Unconscious* and *England, My England* in the fall, after the Lawrences have left England for Australia via Ceylon. Writes most of his novel about Australia (*Kangaroo*), then travels to Taos, New Mexico.

1923   Writes more of *Birds, Beasts and Flowers*, the final version of *Studies in Classic American Literature*, and begins "Quetzalcoatl" (later *The Plumed Serpent*). Travels to Mexico City, Lake Chapala.

1924   In New York with Frieda, who sails for England alone after a quarrel. He returns to Mexico, then joins Frieda in England in October. Travels to Oaxaca, Mexico, by way of France, Germany, and Taos. Continues writing *The Plumed Serpent*. Death of his father.

1925   Taken seriously ill in Mexico, where he is diagnosed as having malaria. Recuperates in Taos while finishing *The Plumed Serpent* and a play, *David*. Returns to England, then travels to Germany and Italy with Frieda. Diagnosed as having tuberculosis.

1926   Lawrence and Frieda settle outside Florence at the Villa Mirenda, where he writes two versions of *Lady Chatterley's Lover*. During the year, visits Germany and England (the latter for the last time).

1927   Back at the Villa Mirenda, Lawrence paints, visits Etruscan tombs and archaeological museums in Italy, and begins *Etruscan Places*.

1928   Writes final version of *Lady Chatterley's Lover*. Visits Germany again; lives in the south of France. Postal authorities seize manuscript of *Pansies*, a new volume of poetry. Writes "Introduction to These Paintings."

1929   In July, his paintings seized in raid on a London museum. Winter spent in Bandol, writing *Nettles* and two works to be published posthumously: *Apocalypse* (1931) and *Last Poems* (1932).

1930   *Nettles* published. Lawrence enters the Ad Astra sanitorium in Vence, France, on 6 February. On 1 March, moved to Villa Robermond. Dies 2 March.

1935   Ashes moved to New Mexico.

1

HISTORICAL CONTEXT

D. H. Lawrence was a poet, a novelist, a philosophical essayist, a playwright, and an author of "travel" books that are really creative works of archaeological scholarship. That he achieved so much in so many zones of the literary realm is testimony to his genius, for Lawrence was also the fourth child of a Nottinghamshire coal miner and his wife. Of all the contexts out of which Lawrence's literary art grew and took shape, his early life in the mining area of Eastwood is probably the most important.

Sons and Lovers, Lawrence's first great novel and the subject of this study, was begun in 1910, finished in 1912, and published in 1913, when Lawrence was twenty-eight years old. Originally entitled "Paul Morel," the novel tells the story of a young man struggling to be an artist in spite of the fact that he has grown up in the mining area called the Bottoms, just down the hill from the town of Bestwood. Paul struggles against the harshness of an environment defined by mines, manufacturing, and all the outward and inward conflicts produced by the industrialization of what had only recently been an agricultural England.

In the novel, Lawrence depicts men who do work that is at once monotonous, meaningless, and dangerous—and who escape their boredom and their fears in pubs that their wives never enter. He tells, too, of the women who are not permitted to venture into the darkness either of the mine or of the pub. We see some of those women doing even more monotonous jobs in factories than their male counterparts do below ground. But there is another kind of woman as well. In Paul's mother, Gertrude, we see a woman much like Lawrence's own mother, Lydia. Gertrude's life is confined neither in an underground shaft nor in a mechanized factory. Its boundaries are marked, rather, by the walls of convention and, more immediately, by the walls of a home that is just like all the other homes built by the mining company for mining families. There she exists with no outlets for love or hope save those provided by her Protestant religion and her talented son. She sees her husband only in the evening, once he has become both drunk and violent.

The area around Eastwood, the town in which D. H. Lawrence was born, had not always been the way Bestwood and vicinity are described in *Sons and Lovers*. In an essay entitled "Nottingham and the Mining Countryside," Lawrence recalls that it was not until "somewhere about 1820" that "B.W. and Co." came along and "sunk the first big [mine] shaft." Before then, some coal had been mined in the region, but there had been no "real industrial colliery"—only a small hole in the ground here and there, each one of which looked like a mere "accident in the landscape, and Robin Hood and his merry men were not very far away." The landscape, back then, was predominantly "agricultural," that is, where it was not defined by dense "forest."[1]

Once the big shafts were sunk in Lawrence's home district, though, many of the trees in Sherwood Forest came down and tiny villages were expanded by the mining companies into sprawling towns. "Most of the little rows of dwellings of the old style miners were pulled down, and dull little shops began to rise," Lawrence writes, "while on the down side [of Eastwood] . . . the company erected" rows of what are "still known as the New Buildings." These buildings, which are still standing today, were the ones Lawrence grew up in. They "consist," Lawrence remarks, of little four-room houses with the "front" looking outward into the grim, blank street, and the "back," with a tiny square brick yard, a low wall, and a w.c. and ash-pit, looking into the desert of the square. . . . The squares [are] quite big, and absolutely desert, save for the posts for clothes lines, and people passing, children playing on the hard earth. . . .

There must be three or four hundred company houses in the squares and the streets that surround the squares, like a great barracks wall. . . . We lived in . . . a corner house.[2]

In *Sons and Lovers* Lawrence describes the same scene in nearly the same terms. He begins the novel by saying that, "sixty years before" the date at which his story commences, the "brook" and "trees" on "Greenhill Lane" were "scarcely soiled by . . . small mines, whose coal was drawn to the surface by donkeys that plodded wearily in a circle round a gin . . . making queer mounds and little black places among the corn-fields and the meadows. And the cottages of these coal-miners . . . together with odd farms and homes . . . straying over the parish, formed the village of Bestwood."[3] But, "some sixty years ago, a sudden change took place. The gin-pits were elbowed aside by the large mines of the financiers. . . . Carston, Waite and Co. appeared . . . on the edge of Sherwood Forest," just "past Robin Hood's well" (1). On the slope below Bestwood, the narrator tells us, in an area that came to be known as the Bottoms, "the Squares" were thrown up. The Squares were houses built in "two rows, . . . twelve houses in a block," with a street on either side of the "double row of dwellings." In each house, on the first floor, there was an "uninhabited parlour" and also the room where families lived, namely, "the kitchen," which "was at the back of the house, facing inward between the blocks, looking at a scrubby back garden, and then at the ash pits. And between the rows, between the long lines of ash-pits, went the alley, where the children played and the women gossiped" (2).

One of the most important influences on *Sons and Lovers*, then, is the town—or the type of town—in which Lawrence himself grew up. Such towns, of course, were the by-product of nineteenth-century industrialism, with its large-scale manufacturing and all-powerful mining and manufacturing companies. Towns like the one Lawrence describes both in fiction and in nonfiction had been "planked down" suddenly on hillsides by such companies, to be inhabited by workers who were abandoning farmland in exchange for an hourly wage.[4] Such environments had not existed in the medieval or Renaissance world that Lawrence alludes to by speaking of Robin Hood and his merry men. That older, feudal world of personal protectors and tyrants had survived in rural pockets of England until bureaucratic bosses and "financiers," as Lawrence calls them, replaced the lord of the manor in the life of common people.

The social, political, and economic changes in England that Lawrence alludes to in "Nottingham and the Mining Countryside" help to explain both the characters and the conflicts described in *Sons and Lovers*. Mr. Morel, one of the three main characters in the novel, is a man of the laboring class. Like Lawrence's father, he speaks the lower-class dialect of the area in which he was born. His wife, like Lawrence's mother, speaks with "a purity of English" that is a marvel to her husband (9). Gertrude Morel is not a product of the lower classes, which is not to say that her nineteenth-century forebears have not known the life of poverty. She is the granddaughter of a man who "had gone bankrupt in the lace-market at a time when so many lace-manufacturers were ruined in Nottingham." She is the daughter of an engineer who, "bitterly galled by" early poverty, had struggled to become "foreman of the engineers in the dockyard at Sheerness" (7). She is, in other words, a member of the doggedly aspiring middle class, which had emerged as feudalism had broken down and as large numbers of workers had been able, for the first time, to dream of what we call upward mobility. Her marital conflicts are to a great extent class conflicts. Her husband, like most nineteenth-century lower-class men, has no religion to speak of. Gertrude, on the other hand, has middle-class religion; she is a zealous member of a Congregational church, which is to say that she is not a member of the ancient Church of England. Her social and religious values are those of self-improvement through good behavior, and her vision of the good life is that of living an orderly life in a nice house. She had not been anxious to move to the house we first meet her in, Lawrence tells us in the novel's seventh paragraph, but at least "she had an end house in one of the top blocks, and thus only one neighbour; on the other side an extra strip of garden. And, having an end house, she enjoyed a kind of aristocracy among the other women of the 'between' houses" (2).

The changes in English society that Lawrence describes, both in *Sons and Lovers* and in "Nottingham and the Mining Countryside," are changes that he is obviously critical of. Lawrence grew up, moreover, in a political environment in which socialism was emerging as a strong new voice, one highly critical of what socialists saw as a capitalist economy out of control. Socialists were speaking out against the depersonalization of life, against the exploitation of men and women by company bosses, and against that newest of tyrants, the monopolistic company. Lawrence knew the socialist viewpoint well. Frank Kermode, in his book entitled *D. H. Lawrence,* says that "Lawrence, obedient to his mother, made good use of the educational provisions of his region." These included "the chapel, the free library, and a flow of visits from great speakers, often exponents of English socialism."[5]

Sons and Lovers certainly would seem to bear out Kermode's view that left-wing political thought counted in Lawrence's early education. Paul, the largely autobiographical hero of the novel, is said to have "more or less got into connection with the Socialist, Suffragette, Unitarian people ... owing to his acquaintance with Clara" (259). Lawrence's correspondence, too, shows at least a cautious interest in political causes and movements. Two years after publishing *Sons and Lovers,* Lawrence struck up a friendship with Bertrand Russell, the mathematician-philosopher whose pacifist views elicited an excited letter from Lawrence advocating the need for political revolution, urging the abolition of private property, and, in Kermode's words, "contemplating action on behalf of the cause he and Russell, briefly, took up. But he told Russell he must drop his [belief in] democracy. 'There must be an aristocracy of people who have wisdom, and there must be a ruler.'"[6] Russell later decided that his own views and Lawrence's were quite different and that Lawrence was closer to being a fascist than a socialist.

But the thinking of many a nineteenth-century radical looks, in retrospect, as if it helped pave the way to national socialism, that is to say, fascism. The German philosopher Friedrich Nietzsche, whose somewhat mystical celebrations of freedom greatly inspired Lawrence, looks in hindsight like a Nazi prophet. Edward Carpenter, a member of the London socialist movement, seems similarly suspect because of a phrase he invented, "blood knowledge." The phrase, which was coined to advocate a kind of redemptive antiintellectualism, also implied anti-Semitism. Lawrence, after Carpenter, used the phrase "blood consciousness" to refer to a revolutionary kind of knowledge. (Lawrence followed Carpenter's lead in other ways as well. Carpenter's books, which include *Civilization: Its Cause and Cure* [1889], *Love's Coming of Age* [1895], and *The Intermediate Sex* [1908], anticipate Lawrence's view that political and sexual conditions are bound up together and that a revolution in one sphere necessitates a revolution in the other.)

Finally, however, to see Lawrence's social criticism in the light of either socialism or fascism is to overlook some important facts as well as some influences on his work that are, in the last analysis, more significant than those of any philosopher—political or otherwise. For one thing, Lawrence's abhorrence of the world of mines and manufacturing was an aesthetic, not a political, attitude. That is to say, Lawrence most objects to what the "company" has done to life in Nottinghamshire not because it is unjust but, rather, because it is ugly. "The great crime which the moneyed classes and promoters of industry committed in the palmy Victorian days was the condemning of the workers to ugliness, ugliness, ugliness: meanness and formless and ugly surroundings, ugly ideals, ugly religion, ugly hope, ugly love, ugly clothes, ugly furniture, ugly houses.... The human soul needs ... beauty even more than bread."[7] Thus, Lawrence is first and foremost an artist in search of beauty, not a political architect in search of a fairer political structure. Even his interest and participation in utopian movements inspired by the American commune leader John Humphrey Noyes were motivated more by the artist's desire to live in a condition of beauty than by the reformer's desire to establish social blueprints for the future.

Historical Context

As an artist, Lawrence was influenced by other artists even more than by political and social philosophers. Although he stood apart, always, from organized movements, he sympathized with many of the interests of the futurists, and he was especially fascinated by the French symbolists, whose richly textured poetry introduced a sensuality to literature that Lawrence felt English writing—and life—sadly lacked. Lawrence's use of writers such as Baudelaire and Verlaine in an effort to reject the influence of British writers such as Scott and Wordsworth will be discussed at length later in this study; suffice it to say here that at one point the conflict between Paul and his first lover, Miriam, is defined in terms of a literary opposition: "She did not like Baudelaire, on the whole—nor Verlaine," Lawrence writes in the "Strife in Love" chapter of the novel:

> "Behold her singing in the field
> Yon solitary highland lass."

That nourished her heart. So did "Fair Ines." And—

> "It was a beauteous evening, calm and pure,
> And breathing holy quiet like a nun."

These were like herself. And there was he, saying . . .
> "*Tu te rappelleras la beauté des caresses.*" (209)

Thomas Hardy, too, was a profound influence on Lawrence. Hardy's sensual appreciation of the rich vitality of earth, together with his cynical views on the institution of marriage, are implicit in *Sons and Lovers* as well as in Lawrence's later, great novels: *The Rainbow* (1915) and *Women in Love* (1920). Indeed, the most important—and only book-length—work Lawrence wrote between *Sons and Lovers* and *The Rainbow* was his 1914 *Study of Thomas Hardy,* in which he is inspired by Hardy to say that "every man comprises male and female in his being. . . . A woman likewise consists in male and female."[8] It is this view that stands at the heart of *Sons and Lovers.*

Because Lawrence is interested in the complex relationship

between male and female, and because of his conviction that the male-female relationship affects and is affected by the inner life, there is another writer who may have influenced Lawrence even more powerfully than Thomas Hardy; namely, Sigmund Freud. It is by no means certain that Lawrence had read Freud by the time he began to write "Paul Morel," the first version of *Sons and Lovers*. We do know, though, that by 1912—the year before the final draft of the novel was produced—Lawrence was arguing about Freud with Frieda, the woman who in 1914 became his wife. Freud's influence over Lawrence's later work, moreover, is indubitable. In 1921, Lawrence published *Psychoanalysis and the Unconscious,* and in 1922 he published *Fantasia of the Unconscious;* both books offer a critique of Freud's psychoanalytic theory, together with Lawrence's own, somewhat different theory about the relationship between conscious and unconscious life. Thus, even if Lawrence had more or less formed the story of *Sons and Lovers* before discovering Freud, it is difficult to avoid connecting Freud with the novel. For one thing, even before he had heard of Freud, Lawrence shared the Austrian physician's interests in gender and unconscious life. Even more important, Lawrence's own ideas seem to have paralleled and even anticipated Freud's. Lawrence may have come, by the 1920s, to object to many of the assumptions and details found in Freud's writings, but in 1912 he penned his own analysis of *Sons and Lovers* in a letter written to a friend, Edward Garnett:

> A woman of character and refinement goes into the lower class, and has no satisfaction in her own life. She has had a passion for her husband. . . . But as her sons grow up, she selects them as lovers. . . . [W]hen they come to manhood, they can't love, because their mother is the strongest power in their lives, and holds them. . . . As soon as the young men come into contact with women there is a split. . . . [A]ll the sons hate and are jealous of the father. The battle goes on between the mother and the girl, with the son as object.[9]

The passage more than suggests that Lawrence's understanding of Paul

Morel and of his problems was very close to Freud's theory of the Oedipal complex. Indeed, it is difficult not to see Freud's influence already at work. The passage also suggests something else, however. Many influences are evident in *Sons and Lovers*. Lawrence's view of psychology cannot be separated from his views on social class and the family, which, as we have seen both in this chapter and in the Chronology, were heavily influenced by his own experiences growing up, in Nottingham and the mining countryside, with a mother "of character and refinement" who had gone down "into the lower class." *Sons and Lovers* is a great novel, but it is also an early novel—a passionate, personal novel by a young man bent on understanding his own life's story.

2

THE IMPORTANCE
OF THE WORK

In *The Dark Sun: A Study of D. H. Lawrence,* Graham Hough views
Sons and Lovers as a psychological novel the importance of which lies
to a great extent not only in its general psychological insights but also,
specifically, in its Freudianism. "*Sons and Lovers* is indeed the first
Freudian novel in English," Hough boldly claims, although "its Freudianism," he admits,

> is mediated not by a text-book but by a person—a person, more-
> over, who was at the same time offering an object-lesson in many
> of the matters with which Freud deals. . . . It cannot be supposed
> that Frieda Lawrence's Freudianism (which is unlikely to have been
> very scholastically complete) materially altered the conception of
> the story, most of which, in any case, was in being before [Frieda]
> came on the scene. What it could and almost certainly did do is set
> a theoretical seal on a situation that had been very thoroughly ex-
> plored in actuality. Its influence can surely be detected in the anal-
> ysis of the novel sent to Garnett.[10]

Hough values the novel not only for its exploration of "the Freudian
Oedipus imbroglio in almost classic completeness" but also because it

is Lawrence's own personal "Oedipus imbroglio" that is being written about. Thus, for Hough, the significance of *Sons and Lovers* lies in the fact that it is a rare act of authorial self-analysis. "*Sons and Lovers* is a special case, and its relation to reality is a peculiar one," Hough writes. "The book is a catharsis, achieved by re-living an actual experience . . . and the achievement is a necessary preliminary to all the later work."[11]

For many of us who enjoy reading Lawrence, however, the real importance of *Sons and Lovers* lies in something other than its Freudianism. Even the fact that the book seems to offer some kind of insight into the author's psychology does not seem of primary importance, since if Lawrence's fiction did not appeal to us on other grounds, we would not care to know about the author's psychology. It is because the book has other significance that we want to know about the man who wrote it. Thus, we may be fascinated to learn, with Hough, that Lawrence put his personal past behind him by writing *Sons and Lovers*, but that fascination is secondary to what we have already felt while experiencing the novel as fiction.

What, then, makes *Sons and Lovers* special and unique? What makes it, in Hough's phrase, a "special case," if not the fact that it is a book whose author has performed in his writing an act of Freudian self-analysis? After all, *Sons and Lovers* does not seem a highly polished novel in the way that James Joyce's *Portrait of the Artist as a Young Man* is an exquisitely wrought work of fiction. Nor does it have the intricate narrative structure of books like *Wuthering Heights* and *Lord Jim*, each of which is a Chinese box of narratives within narratives, the structure of which suggests almost as much as the story itself about the interior life of the characters. Why, then, do we still study *Sons and Lovers* at the end of a century that was still young when it was written?

It is a question that will be further answered in chapters 4 through 7. Suffice it to say here, first, that most of us are probably struck by the almost palpable reality of Lawrence's world. The world of *Sons and Lovers* may be an alternate reality for all of us, but there seems to be more *reality* in it than there is in Emily Brontë's moody moorlands or James Joyce's world of words. Julian Moynahan, in *The Deed of Life: The Novels and Tales of D. H. Lawrence*, points out that Lawrence not only "confronts" the problematical psychological nature of "the mother-son relation" but also "places it at the center of a real world built up through an astonishingly detailed recreation of a complex human environment." We come to feel what it would have been like to live as a man or a woman in the colliery village; we therefore appreciate almost sensually the rich, clean beauty of the Leivers's farm, and we even "come to understand the exact routines of a small Victorian factory. . . . This background is deeply relevant to the central conflicts of the book. It conditions the struggle of some of the characters to realize themselves and helps explain the baffled compromise that other characters make with the circumstances into which they were born. I know of no other English novel, with the possible exception of *Middlemarch*, where people are so rooted in concrete social history, and in a region so concretely rendered."[12]

As we shall see in the next chapter, many critics have valued *Sons and Lovers* either for its psychosexual insights or for the astonishing detail with which the novel represents farms, factories, mines, churches, and the social conventions that govern those places. In his recent book, *Class, Politics, and the Individual: A Study of the Major Works of D. H. Lawrence*, Peter Scheckner states that "generally critics do not credit Lawrence with the understanding that man's sexual and psychological make-up is rooted in a social setting."[13] Scheckner is entirely correct: what most critics have overlooked is the way in which Lawrence reveals the sociological origins of psychosexual traumas.

Sons and Lovers, then, is a successful novel in terms of both its psychological realism and its realistic representations of the external world, including the social world. But the abiding importance of *Sons and Lovers*—the genius of the novel, we might say—does not reside in the psychological explanations it offers for why young men with certain kinds of mothers and fathers may grow up unable to love certain kinds of women. Nor does it lie in the novel's wealth of detail, detail that nonetheless helps us to realize exactly what it would have been like to have worked in a factory in which "surgical appliances" were manufactured—or to have grown up living in a "company town" that was thrown up overnight on a Nottinghamshire hillside. Rather, the book is important because it shows that living and working in a particular environment in a particular time may cause our minds to receive a peculiar warp. A second look at Lawrence's own analysis of *Sons and Lovers* makes this perfectly clear. "A woman of character and refinement," Lawrence wrote, "goes into the lower class, and has no satisfaction in her own life. She has had a passion for her husband. . . . But as her sons grow up, she selects them as lovers."[14] Thus, we may arrive at a deepened appreciation of Lawrence by considering his work in light of psychological theory, but our reading is even more enriched if we remember that Lawrence knew of and wrote about tensions that are not entirely psychological. The passage above clearly grounds the unhealthy relationship between Mrs. Morel and her sons not in the psyche so much as in social tensions, tensions born of industrialization and the emergence of an aspiring middle class. Mrs. Morel's relationship to her boys may be classifiable in terms of Freudian theory, but it is a relationship, Lawrence suggests, that begins with the movement of a "woman of character" into lower-class life.

3

CRITICAL RECEPTION

Some early reviewers suspected strongly that *Sons and Lovers* was an autobiographical work. "We suspect that Paul is a projection of the writer's own personality," Harold Massingham wrote in a 1913 review published in the *Daily Chronicle*.[15] Others did not explicitly make a direct connection between Lawrence and Paul, but they did notice— and object to—the passionately personal style of *Sons and Lovers*. One anonymous reviewer, writing in the *Westminster Gazette*, complained that Lawrence "place[s] more interest on feeling than on action."[16] In another unsigned review, this one published in the *Saturday Review*, "the frequent intrusion of the writer" is said to be "what is wrong in the book. . . . Mr. Lawrence's inability to efface himself is his most serious weakness." The reviewer continues, "The men and women use words which are his and not their own; their reading is in the literature for which he cares; often they express thoughts which belong to him and not to them."[17]

It was 1915, however, before any reviewer fully insisted upon the autobiographical nature of *Sons and Lovers*. "In order to understand Mr. Lawrence fully, we must go beyond his works," Alfred Kuttner suggested in the *New Republic*. Insisting on the strong similarity between *Sons and Lovers* and Lawrence's earlier novels and love poems,

Kuttner declared all these works to be "expressions of the same personal experience," namely, Lawrence's "hatred" for his "father." Having said this, Kuttner went even further, suggesting that what Lawrence "particularizes so passionately" is what Freud, more generally, "has proved beyond cavil," namely, that "the child's attachment to the parent of the opposite sex becomes the prototype of all later love relations."[18]

Apparently certain of the applicability of the Freudian model, Kuttner focused his discussion on the "abnormal concentration" of "love" upon Gertrude Morel.[19] In doing so, Kuttner followed the lead of earlier critics such as Louise Maunsell Field. Although she did not read *Sons and Lovers* as Freudian autobiography, Field described the work in the *New York Times Book Review* as a passionate tribute to "the heroic little mother—the best-drawn character in [the] book."[20]

Other, even earlier reviewers, however, had expressed the view that *Sons and Lovers* offers a more sympathetic portrait of Paul's father. The anonymous critic writing in the *Saturday Review* had argued that "the young [Morel] family grows up zealous for the mother; but with the touch of skill Mr. Lawrence can show the father as the good fellow whom these others never know."[21] An unsigned 1913 review in the *Standard* suggested that "the wastage of the best in humanity is the keynote of the book" and that Walter Morel the coal miner, not his wife, offers the saddest example of the wasted life. "The growing children are always on the side of the mother, yet we know that the father is in many ways a good fellow . . . running to waste."[22]

What we find, then, in the early reviews of *Sons and Lovers* is what we would expect to find: a variety of attitudes toward and assessments of a book by a relative newcomer to the literary scene. Some of Lawrence's contemporaries insisted on seeing the novel as the author's only-slightly-revised personal history; others did not, although one complained about the writer's lack of "scientific detachment."[23] Some of the reviewers believed the book to be about the tragic "wastage" of Walter Morel; others thought the author was writing against his own, biological father. Then, too, there were critics who seemed to sense that the inconsistent reviews of the book were made possible by the work itself, which is about emotional oxymorons, passionate contradictions. As Lascelles Abercrombie pointed out, *Sons and Lovers* is a novel that makes us "look for the word 'hate' as soon as we have read the word 'love.' . . . Life, for Mr. Lawrence, is a coin that has both obverse and reverse; so it is for most people."[24] Most people, in other words, have both loved and hated fathers and mothers because they were or seemed, alternately, lovable and hateworthy. Behavior changes and loyalties ebb and swell, often unpredictably.

Even as he praised the truthfulness of *Sons and Lovers*, however, Abercrombie, like so many of Lawrence's contemporaries, attacked the novel for having "no particular shape and no recognizable plot." He called it a work in which "themes are casually taken up, and then as casually dropped," whereas "there seems no reason why they should have been taken up unless they were to be kept up."[25] We may ask: how could a reviewer praise Lawrence for telling a lifelike story about the changeability and contradictoriness of life and, at the same time, decry the novel's lack of definite, consistent shape and form?

It is a question worth asking, for the interpretive history of *Sons and Lovers* is the history of critics trying to claim that the book is at once autobiographical and artistic. If it is autobiographical, we would expect it to have a somewhat haphazard story line, as well as a somewhat involved, even intrusive, narrator. If, on the other hand, it is a product of novelistic art, then it must have been shaped by a craftsman who has given it definite or even symmetrical form and consistent meanings that are suggested and undergirded by form. If *Sons and Lovers* is that kind of crafted, formal arrangement of words, then it is not the story of any real man's life, and we may certainly not perform a Freudian analysis of D. H. Lawrence by reading it. (We probably cannot psychoanalyze Paul, either, for he is a constructed character, not a complete human psyche.) If Lawrence, however, has simply projected his mind and life onto the page, then the novel may be too unprocessed, too unshaped, to be discussed and analyzed as novelistic art.

If there were doubts, initially, about whether *Sons and Lovers* had an autobiographical basis, they disappeared in 1935, when Jessie

Chambers published *D. H. Lawrence: A Personal Record* under the pseudonymic initials "E. T." In her book, Chambers claimed she was the prototype for the character Miriam and stated unequivocally that in writing the novel Lawrence had been writing the story of his own struggle toward manhood.[26] Richard Aldington, who wrote the first biographical study of Lawrence, later called Chambers not only the "Miriam of *Sons and Lovers*" but also "the Emily of *The White Peacock*" and the "heroine of several early stories," thus suggesting that all Lawrence's early works are autobiographical. In *D. H. Lawrence: Portrait of a Genius But . . .*, Aldington tells how Jessie Chambers made "notes . . . about their early life together," which Lawrence requested before attempting to revise an early draft of *Sons and Lovers* entitled "Paul Morel."[27] Indeed, Aldington goes so far in assuming that Lawrence's fiction was also his life's story that he assumes Lawrence to have earned a pound a week the year before entering University College, Nottingham, because that is how much money Paul Morel made![28] More convincingly, he quotes Frieda as saying that Lawrence "suffered" while writing the final draft of the book, especially "when he came to the point when he had to re-live his mother's illness and death."[29]

Aldington was more of a biographer than a literary critic. F. R. Leavis, however, who published a landmark critical study of Lawrence five years after Aldington's biography (which appeared in 1950) agreed entirely with Aldington's view of *Sons and Lovers* as thinly disguised autobiography. *The Rainbow* and *Women in Love* are Lawrence's great achievements, according to Leavis. "This is not to dismiss *Sons and Lovers*," Leavis writes, but rather to say that the earlier novel is an outgrowth of its author's own "emotional life," a "direct and wholly convention-free treatment of the personal problem."

> With *Sons and Lovers* Lawrence put something behind him . . . for good. The acute emotional problem or disorder which queered his personal relations and the play of his intelligence has been placed— has been conquered—by intelligence. . . . He is now freed for the work of the greatest kind of artist.

> It is *The Rainbow* and *Women in Love* . . . that prove him to
> be that.[30]

Later in his study, which was entitled *D. H. Lawrence: Novelist,*
Leavis calls *Women in Love* "the work of the writer who, in under-
taking *The Rainbow,* had explained that another *Sons and Lovers*
must not be looked for from him [because] the original treatment of
life he was now proposing required a formidable originality of method
and style."[31] Leavis thus tries to write his way around the central question that had been posed about the novel, namely: "it's an interesting
insight into Lawrence's troublesome early life, but is it good art?"
Leavis simply suggests that *Sons and Lovers* was the overly personal
book that Lawrence needed to write in order to transcend himself, in
order to achieve the artistic disengagement that makes *The Rainbow*
and *Women in Love* better novels.

Graham Hough, a British Freudian critic who was a contemporary of Leavis, follows his lead. Hough, whose book *The Dark Sun*
was the first thoroughgoing critical study of Lawrence's fiction and
poetry, begins by insisting that *Sons and Lovers* is highly autobiographical. He reminds readers that the character of Miriam "was created under the direct supervision of her actual prototype [Jessie
Chambers]" and that "the whole of the 'Lad and Girl Love' chapter
. . . may have been written from notes supplied by her." As for the
"whole situation" Paul and his mother find themselves in, it not only
"presents the Freudian Oedipus imbroglio in almost tragic completeness," but it is also the tragic situation that Lawrence and his mother
Lydia found themselves in. To prove what by 1956 hardly needed
proving, he quotes Jessie Chambers. "The day before his mother's fu-
neral," Chambers wrote, "we went [on] a walk together. . . ."

> [H]e said to me:
>   "You know, J., I've always loved mother."
>   "I know you have," I replied.
>   "I don't mean that," he answered. "I've loved her—like a
> lover—that's why I could never love you."[32]

Hough, like Leavis before him, maintains that Lawrence was too personally involved with the story of Paul and Gertrude Morel to make good art out of it. Just as the first reviewers felt the novelist played too "intrusive" a part in his characters' thoughts and words—especially those of Paul—so Hough thinks that Lawrence, for autobiographical reasons, "is identifying himself too closely with Paul's point of view."[33] But a flawed novel, Hough observes, can still be an interesting and even powerful book, especially when it was written by a writer who went on to produce great works of art. For Hough, as for Leavis, *Sons and Lovers* is the workshop in which Lawrence put his personal trauma behind him and learned to write novels: "*Sons and Lovers* is a special case, and its relation to reality is a curious one. The book is a catharsis, achieved by re-living an actual experience . . . and the achievement is a necessary preliminary to all the later work."[34] *Sons and Lovers* is interesting, then, because it is "the first Freudian novel in English," by which Hough means that the novel was Lawrence's "means of coming to understand a situation where understanding has not been achieved in ordinary experience."[35]

Several important critics writing about Lawrence during the 1940s and 1950s, then, tended to appreciate *Sons and Lovers* in spite of what they saw as its lack of technique and artistry. Two critics, however, Mark Schorer and Mark Spilka, were unwilling to make the assumption that technique and form are not to be expected in an autobiographical novel of Freudian self-analysis and self-transcendence. Nor were they willing to value *Sons and Lovers* merely because it was a novel in which Lawrence wrote his way through traumatic personal problems and toward an era in which he would write well. Schorer, in an article entitled "Technique as Discovery" (1948), doubts that Lawrence did write his way through his problems in *Sons and Lovers*. He finds, from beginning to end, an unresolved discrepancy between the novel's treatment of two themes ("the crippling effects of a mother's love . . . and the 'split' between kinds of love, as represented by . . . Clara and Miriam"). He suggests that there is a similar discrepancy, moreover, between Lawrence's various treatments of the two parental characters.[36] Schorer insists that Lawrence never shows the relationship between Gertrude's love for her son and the "split" between Paul's physical and spiritual longings, and he also insists that, "at the same time the book condemns the mother, it justifies her."[37] This "psychological tension . . . disrupts the form" and "style" of the novel throughout, according to Schorer; it leads to a devastating "contradiction" between "expressed moral epithets and the more general texture of the prose." It leads, as well, to a contradiction in "point of view."[38]

In contradistinction to critics such as Leavis and Hough, Schorer argues that only by crafting an artistically consistent and integrated work, that only by distancing himself from his story via the impersonality of formal artistic technique, could Lawrence have put this personal trauma behind him. "[M]erely to look into one's heart and write," Schorer insists, "is also merely to repeat the round of emotional bondage. If our books are to be exercises in self-analysis," he continues, "then technique must . . . take the place of the absent analyst."[39]

Mark Spilka, like Schorer, argues that "self-discovery" depends upon technique. Like Schorer, too, he admits that *Sons and Lovers* is a divided novel. Unlike Schorer, however, he views the division as a relatively insignificant one that does not preclude the novel's having a definite artistic form. Thus, unlike Schorer, he believes that in writing *Sons and Lovers* Lawrence not only created, through technique, a work of art, but also came to terms with his own past.

In *The Love Ethic of D. H. Lawrence* (1955), Spilka agrees with Schorer that "there are *two* psychologies that work in *Sons and Lovers*." One of these, which is Freudian, wants to blame Gertrude Morel for Paul's failed romances with Miriam and Clara Dawes. The other "psychology," however, is anti-Freudian; it holds that the love between Paul and Miriam is doomed by abstraction, even as the love between Paul and Clara is doomed by Clara's "inadequacy as an independent being."[40] This latter "psychology" sees the "companionship between mother and sons" as "wholesome" at first. (Gertrude's sons, Spilka argues, are "kindled to life" by their mother, who provides "the delightful quality" of their lives.) Even late in the novel, according to Spilka, this "psychology" of Lawrence shows us "relations between

Paul and his mother" that "are sometimes rich in satisfaction." Lawrence's anti-Freudian psychology admits to the Oedipal nature of certain moments in the mother-son relationship, but the novel is finally about three unrelated but equally "destructive forms of love—oedipal, spiritual, and 'unbalanced-possessive.' "[41]

Julian Moynahan, like Mark Spilka, cannot deny the presence of a psychology at once "Freudian" and Lawrence's own. In *The Deed of Life* (1963), he states that "[Paul] is trapped in a pattern of 'repetition compulsion' from which there is no escape this side of the analyst's couch." Arguing that Frieda had read Freud—and submitting that Lawrence probably had—before the final draft of *Sons and Lovers* was completed, Moynahan suggests that "Lawrence's construction of a sort of neurotic case history for Paul is both accurate and comprehensive"—this in spite of the fact that Lawrence later "took issue with Freudians on two points: on the primacy of the sexual impulse" and on "the value of bringing neurotics to a conscious awareness of repressed instincts and drives."[42] This hardly means, however, that Lawrence's psychological outlook is what makes the novel matter. Nor, Moynahan goes on to say, does the presence of other psychologies or themes make the novel formless, as so many earlier critics assumed.

Somewhat as Spilka saw the novel focusing on three different forms of love, Moynahan finds "three formal orders or matrices" that define the deep structure of *Sons and Lovers*. These matrices interlock, "blend with," and "enrich" one another. "The first matrix is autobiographical narrative," the second is a narrative "taken over from psychoanalytic theory," whereas the third is a narrative advancing an attitude that Moynahan calls "vitalism." Finally, the indeterminacy of the novel is resolved as the autobiographical narrative weakens and as the "vitalism of the novel, which do[es] not coincide" with the Freudian matrix, triumphs over it.[43] By Lawrence's "vitalism," Moynahan means a belief that the human self cannot finally be determined by outside, environmental forces, the belief that "passional" being is good and that only dispassionate, life-denying being is evil. It is only through "passional or vital logic," finally, that we may judge each character. In a scene like the following, therefore, we can only judge Paul's father negatively, according to Moynahan. "And that was how he tried to dismiss her," Lawrence writes of Walter Morel, late in the novel, after the death of Gertrude. "He never thought of her personally. Everything deep in him he denied. Paul hated his father for sitting sentimentalizing."[44]

Moynahan, then, continues the trend begun by Spilka away from seeing the novel as a passionately confused autobiographical work and toward the view that the autobiographical narrative is only one of several formally counterpointed voices. In *The Forked Flame* (1965), H. M. Daleski furthered the work of Moynahan and Spilka. In Daleski's view, the autobiographical voice (which Daleski simply calls "Lawrence") damns the father and praises the mother, while the artistic voice does the opposite. Thus, "in a way apparently not realized by Lawrence," Mr. Morel's "warmth and exuberance" are positively contrasted with "Mrs. Morel's martyred self-righteousness."[45] Later, Daleski says that although the autobiographical "Lawrence" shows "Morel to be factually responsible" for a particular attack on his wife, the artist shows that "moral responsibility for the clash is Mrs. Morel's. . . . Yet in the scene in which Morel takes himself off to the Palmerston it is implied that blame for the incident attaches to him alone. It is very much as if Lawrence shirks the conclusions of his own art."[46] Finally, however, it is the very counterbalance between views and voices—those of Lawrence the man and Lawrence the artist—that makes *Sons and Lovers* worth reading. Like Spilka and Moynahan, Daleski resists the notion that the conflicts between elements in *Sons and Lovers* make the novel chaotic and confused. Rather, he suggests, invoking William Empson's concept of essential ambiguity, they make for an arresting work of art.

With the publication of Keith Sagar's 1966 book *The Art of D. H. Lawrence,* the era of reading *Sons and Lovers* autobiographically was all but ended. Sagar says that "there is ample evidence" that Lawrence was "mature" by the time he wrote the novel, and argues that "too close a concentration on the autobiographical, the personal problem has persistently led critics away from the novel's value as a work of art and towards its interest as a case history." Sagar implicitly blames Jessie Chambers for getting the interpretive history of *Sons and Lovers* off on the wrong track: "In *A Personal Record* Jessie Chambers epitomizes this non-literary criticism," he writes. Sagar admits that Chambers made clear to her readers that Lawrence "deviated" from the "truth" in writing the novel, but he points out that it never occurred to her that Lawrence was at such moments sacrificing the significance of "truth" to arrive at the "significant form" that characterizes any serious work of art.[47] Sagar follows Spilka's lead in suggesting that Mrs. Morel "gives more [to her sons] than she receives. It is not until she is dying that she begins to sap Paul's life," Sagar writes, thus resisting the temptation to read in Freudian terms as well as the temptation to read autobiographically.[48] Sagar, like Spilka, thus propelled Lawrence criticism toward the day in which *Sons and Lovers* was to be studied for its significant form—and for what that form reflects not of the inner world of D. H. Lawrence but of the world that shaped him.

The 1940s and 1950s were years in which *Sons and Lovers* was read autobiographically by critics barely willing to admit that the novel was crude art. The 1960s saw the publication of books that suggested that personal novels must be artistic if their authors are to grow in self-understanding through the act of writing them. Consequently, many of the critics of the 1960s developed complex models of the novel's "significant form."

By the 1970s the interpretive history of *Sons and Lovers* was, once again, evolving in a new way. The so-called New Criticism—which insisted that art is form and structure—had become moribund, and the advent of sociological, especially Marxist and feminist, criticism was sending a new generation of critics back to Lawrence's fiction to see how well—or poorly—Lawrence revealed the disturbing social truths of his time and nation. Scott Sanders, in *D. H. Lawrence: The World of the Five Major Novels,* suggested that "although it is easy to describe the underlying social matrix which binds together the people and places of the novel's world, Lawrence generally ignored the social existence of his characters, as if some astigmatism had blinded him to the historical forces at work in their lives. The conflict between the father and mother, for example, which is clearly grounded in class differences, is translated into moral terms."[49] According to Sanders, the ideology of the novel is not that of a social critic seeking to explain the conditions of his society; it is, rather, the middle-class Christian ideology of Paul's mother. Her "responses to people, her ideas, her categories of judgment, even her metaphors creep into Paul's speech, and they permeate the narrative description of her thought." Thus the narrative never can reveal the "reasons" for Walter Morel's "drinking." It can only speak of his "ruin and of his wife's bitter suffering."[50]

Peter Scheckner, in *Class, Politics, and the Individual* (1985), carried on the work of Sanders, both by focusing on Lawrence's social criticism and by admitting that it is the lack thereof that characterizes *Sons and Lovers*. Like Sanders, Scheckner says that "*Sons and Lovers* does not go . . . far in rejecting the values of Lawrence's mother and her bourgeois supremacy." Scheckner, however, credits Lawrence for having gone considerably further than Sanders thought he did. Lawrence "reserves for workers a unique dignity," Scheckner writes.[51] Thus, Lawrence's social vision, in Scheckner's view, is not so skewed by bourgeois supremacist notions when the male coal miners are on view. Indeed, "Lawrence describes a conflict between the instinctual, communal life of the men, and the more material aspirations of the women. The men worked," the novel shows, "and the wives aspired to escape the drudgery of the working class life." Work puts Walter Morel in touch with his own people, and in depicting the father, therefore, Lawrence reveals the conditions of the people of his time and place. Since "the women could share in none of this [work]," their minds sought "detachment," and in representing their desire for detachment Lawrence tends to speak their language. Since both the "male" communal and the "female" escapist languages are to be found in *Sons and Lovers*, the novel manages to say something incisive about class and gender division. It says, for instance, that "detached from . . . work itself," women "began to boss their husbands in a way that resembled the social system of workers and owners."[52]

Critical Reception

Feminist criticism in many ways became the most significant form of criticism during the 1980s. Feminist critics might not agree entirely with Scheckner's point of view; on the other hand, they share his essentially socio-critical orientation. Feminist critics, however, have turned back to Lawrence's biography and to biographical readings of *Sons and Lovers*, perhaps because, for them, Lawrence's relationship with his mother cannot be divorced from his views on men and women in society. In *D. H. Lawrence and the Devouring Mother: The Search for a Patriarchal Ideal of Leadership* (1984), Judith Ruderman suggests that Lawrence's simultaneously sympathetic and critical attitudes toward his own mother relate closely to both his true understanding of and his mythic fiction about the male-female relationship. "Works like *Sons and Lovers* suggest that Lawrence realized how deadly it is for a woman to be limited to the care of home and children, and how this deadliness might lead to the . . . smothering of children (and husbands). . . . But in his later, leadership works, Lawrence firmly and unapologetically places woman in her narrow realm," telling men and women with all "the powerful force of myth" that it is the place of men to "do important manly tasks" and the work of women "to refresh and energize them during the interludes that lie between herculean labors."[53]

It is important for us to have a sense of Lawrence's later works. It is equally important, however, for us to appreciate some of the ways in which *Sons and Lovers* is an unusual novel. As the next five chapters suggest, *Sons and Lovers* is unique in part because, unlike other novels by Lawrence and even other novels of its time, it shows how deadly the smothering of women can be, not only for women themselves but also for children and husbands.

A Reading

4

OPPOSITION AND CONFLICT
Gertrude and Walter Morel

The last two critics discussed in the previous chapter differ somewhat in ideology and emphasis. The views of Peter Scheckner, unlike those of Judith Ruderman, are neither feminist nor psychological in their orientation, and whereas Ruderman focuses on women in Lawrence's fiction, Scheckner is interested in the communal life of the men. Both critics, though, see *Sons and Lovers* in terms of conflict—specifically, male-female conflict—and both are interested in the social bases of conflict. Scheckner sees women pitted, like the male managers they can never be, against their own working-class husbands, while Ruderman analyzes the "deadly smothering of women" by a male-dominated society.

My contention is that *Sons and Lovers* is characterized by a conflict between male and female that goes on within several of the novel's characters as well as among almost all of them. External conflicts between individuals often involve, in a triangle, a pair of opposed characters plus a third, radically self-divided one. These tense, triangular relationships not only give impetus to the plot but also provide a formal pattern or structure that supports everything from the novel's symbolic colors and images to its most profound ideas.

The seminal opposition in the novel is, of course, the one that pits Gertrude Morel against her husband, for it is that opposition that is responsible for Paul Morel's deep and destructive self-division. Consideration of the parental opposition and conflict begins, moreover, with the study of Gertrude Morel, for if she is the novel's primary example of what Ruderman calls "the deadly smothering of women," she is also, in many ways, the most important character in the book. (This is true even though her son Paul is not only the protagonist of the novel but also a fictional version of the young D. H. Lawrence.) No sooner has Lawrence described the setting of the novel—the coal-mining fields of Nottinghamshire that lie "on the edge of Sherwood Forest"—than he begins to characterize the mother of the "sons" referred to in his novel's title (1).

We can see from Lawrence's first description of Gertrude that she is a proud and independent-minded woman, one who is, not surprisingly, lonely and dissatisfied with her life in the dirty, male-dominated world of a coal-mining village. When we meet her for the first time, she is at her new home in "the Bottoms," which she enjoys only because it is the "end house" on a long row of identical miners' dwellings. "[H]aving an end house," Lawrence tells us, "she enjoyed a kind of aristocracy among the other women of the 'between' houses. . . . But this superiority in station was not much consolation to Mrs. Morel." Her "new" house, after all, is only new to her; although it is only twelve years old, it is already on "the downward path." Worse yet, Gertrude feels imprisoned in the house, for she is thirty-one, the mother of two small children, pregnant with a third, and married to a man with no ambition to better himself (2).

Only a few pages further into the novel, we see Gertrude home "alone" with her children, William and Annie, waiting for her husband, Walter. He is still at the "wakes," a fair at which miners get drunk while their wives take their children from one tawdry sideshow to another. From the garden just outside her door, she watches women and children "coming home from the wakes. . . . Occasionally a man lurched past," and "sometimes a good husband came along with his family, peacefully. But usually the women and children were alone."

Other women we are to meet in the novel seem relatively insensitive to the injustice of being abandoned by hard-drinking men, but Mrs. Morel—who expects people and places to be "good"—feels deeply oppressed by her situation and environment. "The world seemed a dreary place" to her, a place in which "nothing else" could possibly "happen for her— . . . nothing but this dreary endurance—till the children grew up. And the children! She could not afford to have this third. She did not want it. The father was . . . in a public house, swilling himself drunk. She despised him, and was tied to him. This coming child was too much for her. . . . [S]he was sick of it, the struggle with poverty and ugliness and meanness" (5). The last five words of this passage are telling. Gertrude Morel is a woman with economic, aesthetic, and moral standards and aspirations. She despises lowness in all forms; she would like to have a higher income and live in a beautiful world with a "good" husband, next to refined neighbors. Since she does not, she longs for change—change that her husband is unlikely to bring about and that she is impotent to bring about for herself.

Mrs. Morel comes to realize her powerlessness as she watches a drunk young man crash into a stile at the edge of the road. Lawrence subtly allows the reader to watch this scene through Mrs. Morel's discriminating, even judgmental, eyes as he describes the fellow "pick[ing] himself up" and "swearing viciously, rather pathetically, as if he thought the stile had wanted to hurt him." We know that Mrs. Morel finds the scene pathetic, the sound of swearing vicious, because the combination sends her immediately "indoors, wondering if things were never going to alter. She was beginning to realize that they would not." She wonders what she has "to do with all this"; "it doesn't seem as if *I* were taken into account," she thinks to herself. "I wait," she says to herself, "and what I wait for can never come" (6).

Lawrence begins his novel, then, by picturing a lonely woman who has not only high, unreachable goals but also a degree of understanding and self-knowledge that make her condition extremely painful. That is to say, Gertrude knows that what she waits for can never come. The fact that she continues wanting what she knows she can never have may make her seem somewhat pretentious, smug, and unrealistic. She is a dreamer whose dreams make her despise the shortcomings of others, whether they be young men tripping over stiles or mothers who, unlike herself, are content to "gossip . . . at the corners of the alley . . . folding their arms" stoically "under their white aprons." Next to such women, Gertrude seems "frail"—physically and psychologically. "The heat suffocated her. And looking ahead, the prospect of her life made her feel as if she were buried alive." And she may even seem somewhat self-indulgent as she stands alone in her garden feeling sorry for herself, "trying to soothe herself with the scent of flowers and the fading, beautiful evening" (5). Even nature seems somehow not good enough for her, not quite beautiful enough to offer adequate solace or consolation.

Lawrence, who provides us with pairs of characters who possess opposite strengths and opposite weaknesses, is both critical of and sympathetic with Mrs. Morel, who is, as we have seen, a literary character modeled after his own mother. He is sympathetic, in part, because he knows that all human character is to some extent a given, something present from birth and unalterable. It is difficult enough for human beings to be other than what they have been raised to be, but it is virtually impossible to suspend aspects of identity that have been genetically inherited.

Mrs. Morel is the beneficiary—and victim—of both her social and her biological inheritance. She "came of a good old burgher [middle class] family, famous independents who had fought with Colonel Hutchinson, and who remained stout Congregationalists," the narrator tells us. Such families teach certain values, but they also seem to pass along such characteristics as ambition, willfulness, and rigidity. Certainly, Gertrude's father was born with just such characteristics, which Gertrude seems to have inherited as surely as she inherited her mother's physical traits. George Coppard "was an engineer," the novel tells us: "a large, handsome, haughty man, proud of his fair skin and blue eyes, but more proud still of his integrity. Gertrude resembled her mother in her small build. But her temper, proud and unyielding, she had from the Coppards" (7). Lawrence thus uses the word *proud* three times (and its synonym *haughty* once) in describing the character of George and Gertrude Coppard. When he says that the daughter "had" her pride from her father, he clearly suggests that she inherited as well as learned her father's temper.

Thus, although Lawrence at times criticizes Gertrude's temperament and inner nature—although he shows us that her pride and integrity cause a great deal of suffering—he also understands that this young woman has not chosen her nature. She is not just indulging a passing whim to dream impossible dreams; the dissatisfaction that Gertrude Morel feels with life in the Bottoms has been virtually fated by her background and makeup. After all, her father, too, had felt "bitterly galled by his own poverty." Gertrude may have "favoured her mother" physically, and even "loved her . . . best of all; but she had the Coppard's clear, defiant blue eyes and their broad brow" (7). And that brow, the narrator makes us realize, is more than just a physical characteristic. It is an outward sign of that which lies unalterable at her inner core: a proud, willful, unyielding inner spirit.

The fact that Gertrude Morel is like her father in all but outward appearance is extremely important to *Sons and Lovers,* for perhaps the most important idea set forth by the novel is this: the traits that a given society defines as "male" and "female" are not always to be found in biologically male and female bodies. The world is dreary, suffocating, and unfulfilling indeed for a woman like Gertrude, who has inherited traits that can most usefully be used in playing a man's social part. If Gertrude's father, George, was "bitterly galled at his poverty," how much more galled must his daughter be? George was prevented neither by lack of educational opportunity nor by society's expectations of parents and spouses from becoming an engineer, from trying to better his standard of living. His "gentle, humorous, kindly-souled" wife may have been perfectly content to let her proud and independent husband struggle for her family's betterment. But Gertrude cannot be so content, for she is her father's spirit in her mother's body. And her husband, who has a male body like her father's, has nothing like her father's spirit. He would not, could not, struggle for his family's betterment, even if Gertrude were willing to sit back and let him.

Gertrude is, in addition to being proud, unyielding, and independent, "intellectual" and "spiritual" (as opposed to physical and sensual). Because she is intellectual by nature, she is not only "curious" but also argumentative, especially when the subjects of God and religion come up. Thus, although her curiosity causes her to find "much pleasure and amusement in listening to other folk," she is also "clever in leading folk to talk. She loved ideas," and "what she liked most of all was an argument on religion or philosophy or politics with some educated man." Such talks, unfortunately, "she did not often enjoy," for educated men did not regularly meet to discuss ideas with women in Lawrence's day. "So she always had people tell her about themselves, finding her pleasure so" (9).

The one man she can, occasionally, discuss ideas with is Mr. Heaton, the "young, and very poor" Congregational clergyman who has come to the Bottoms to minister to the miners and their families after receiving his "Bachelor of Arts at Cambridge." Occasionally he called, stayed to tea with Mrs. Morel, and "for hours he talked to her."

> Then she laid the cloth early, got out her best cups . . . and hoped [her husband] would not come too soon; indeed, if he stayed for a pint, she would not mind this day. . . . Mr. Heaton would hold the baby, whilst Mrs. Morel beat up a batter-pudding or peeled the potatoes, and he, watching her all the time, would discuss his next sermon. His ideas were quaint and fantastic. (33)

Even with Mr. Heaton, however, Gertrude has to do more listening than talking; "For hours he talked *to* her," Lawrence makes pointedly clear. He comes to "discuss his next sermon"; her role is to bring him "judiciously to earth" (33, italics mine). Thus, the "curious" side of her intellectual nature is satisfied far more often than the "clever" one. Gertrude is forced to be a listener. When Mr. Heaton comes, she gets to listen and respond to quaint and fantastic ideas. The rest of the time she must listen to what every other woman must content herself with: the details of personal, familial, domestic lives.

Although Lawrence says that Gertrude finds "her pleasure so," he means that she finds what pleasure she finds in listening. That is not to say that she finds a great deal of pleasure, this "lady" who is "considered very intellectual" and who speaks with "a purity of English" that is seldom heard in the Bottoms or in the thatched houses of neighboring "Hell Row." For she is not, by nature, a listener; she is not, by genes and by background, what she must, as a woman, be: receptive and sympathetic. She is, after all, "puritan, like her father." He was a "rather bitter" man "who preferred theology in reading, and who drew near in sympathy only to one man, the Apostle Paul." To Gertrude "her father was . . . the type of all men," and so was Paul, the apostle who was "harsh in government, and in familiarity ironic" (10).

Like her father and like Saint Paul (who in addition to being harsh and ironic "ignored all sensuous pleasure"), Gertrude by nature is "high-minded, and really stern" (10). In characterizing Gertrude, Lawrence repeatedly uses adjectives that describe socially acceptable male—but unacceptable female—characteristics. Gertrude is not only "stern," but she is also "cold," "hard," and "rigid." She sits "rigid with bitterness," for instance, when her husband reveals that he has not yet paid off his wedding bills. She "[is] her father," suddenly, when her mother-in-law reveals that Walter has lied about owning a house. "Then we ought to be paying you rent," she pronounces "coldly," and shortly thereafter "something in her proud, honourable soul . . . crystallise[s] out hard as rock" (12, 13). Not long after that, "a battle" begins "between husband and wife," one in which Gertrude struggles "to make him undertake . . . responsibilities, to make him fulfil his obligations. But he was too different from her. His nature was purely sensuous, and she strove to make him moral, religious. She tried to force him to face things" (14). Gertrude is inevitably disappointed with her husband's lack of "grit." She has grit, and a sense of obligation or responsibility to go with it, but a woman's grit goes unused and unappreciated outside the household. Men "force" women—not vice versa—in the world into which Gertrude has been born, the world she can no more revolutionize in a short lifetime than she can entirely change her own proud, willful nature.

Lawrence beautifully illustrates the not uncommon tension caused both within and between individuals by society's definitions of proper "male" and "female" behavior when he provides a flashback, in chapter 1, to Gertrude Morel's nineteenth year. Back then, four years before meeting Morel, "She used to walk home from chapel with John Field . . . the son of a well-to-do tradesman," who "had been to college in London" and who was planning to take a job in "business." All her life she was to "recall in detail a September Sunday afternoon, when they had sat under the vine at the back of her father's house." It was on that day that she had challenged him:

> "Now sit still," he had cried. "Now your hair, I don't know what it *is* like! It's as bright as copper and gold. . . ."
> She had met his brilliant eyes, but her clear face scarcely showed the elation that rose within her.
> "But you say you don't like business," she pursued.
> "I don't. I hate it!" he cried hotly.
> "And you would like to go into the ministry," she half implored.
> "I should. I should love it, if I thought I could make a first-rate preacher."
> "Then why don't you—why *don't* you?" Her voice rang with defiance. "If *I* were a man, nothing would stop me."
> She held her head erect. He was rather timid before her.
> "But my father's so stiff-necked. He means to put me into the business, and I know he'll do it."
> "But if you're a *man?*" she had cried.
> "Being a man isn't everything," he replied, frowning with puzzled helplessness. (8)

Lawrence has carefully chosen his words to show that both of these young people are to be hindered by traits other than those favored in their gender. In characterizing John Field, Lawrence uses words and phrases and tones that we conventionally associate with femininity ("he had cried," "he cried hotly," "he replied . . . with puzzled helplessness"). The language of the passage, then, shows us that John is as unlike his father, who is "stiff-necked" and who "do[es]" what he "means to," as Gertrude is unlike her sweet and gentle mother. Gertrude, on the other hand, would make a man such as John Field's father a fitting son. In challenging John, "she pursue[s]" him. Her voice "r[ings] with defiance" as she tells him that if she were a man, nothing would stop her. Gertrude is everything John's father is, everything his father would like a son to be. Lawrence even uses words associated with male anatomy to suggest the paradoxical difference between "hard," "rigid" Gertrude and the softer, more compliant John. "[E]lation . . . rose within her" when she heard him poetically wonder at the color of her hair, and she "held her head erect," causing him to be "timid before her." The word *erect*, if nothing else, associates Gertrude with John's "stiff-necked," insistent father.

Unfortunately, as a woman, Gertrude cannot do all the things she "means to," which is why she needs a husband or sons through whom to accomplish her goals. Lawrence sympathizes with those needs, and yet he knows what havoc they can wreak in the life of a mate—especially in the life of a man who, like John Field, was born with the soft, sensitive, acquiescent spirit that society rewards only in a woman. Fortunately for Field, his relationship with Gertrude is interrupted by economic circumstances that force both the Field and the Coppard families to move away from the town of Sheerness. Thanks to a typically "determined" effort, Gertrude manages to find John two years after their separation, but by then he has "married his landlady, a woman of forty, a woman with property." He has been insulated from that zone of reality in which human beings born biologically male usually have to live and move and have their being. He will not have to face the trials of ambition, challenge, success, and failure of the kind that "ruined" even his determined father (8).

Unlike John—and unlike Walter, the man she eventually marries—Gertrude wishes to control life rather than to be controlled by it. She fears feeling helpless, and in contrast to the drunken, happy-go-lucky men who stumble through the streets around her in an alcoholic haze, she is supremely conscious and self-conscious. Her mind dislikes fogginess and, especially, darkness, the unknown that it cannot fathom completely, and Gertrude seldom relaxes her mind enough to enjoy the physical side of life—or life as it simply happens. Lawrence subtly illustrates Gertrude's willfulness, her self-consciousness, and her almost obsessive fear of all she cannot mentally control when he describes her taking her little girl, Annie, down to the brook in the meadows, where "water ran quickly over stones." From that vantage point, she can see the "dipping-hole, at the other end of the meadow," where boys go swimming daily. She can see their "naked forms . . . flashing round the deep" water, an "occasional bright figure dart glittering over the blackish stagnant meadow." She knows that her son William is "at the dipping-hole," and it is the "dread of her life" that he might be someday "drowned" (21).

Only a few pages after describing Gertrude's fearful, distant apprehension of boys who are diving, careless and naked, into the dark depths of water, Lawrence provides us with an even more powerful scene, one that sums up Gertrude's character and provides the reader with a set of terms and images and colors and other symbols that will be associated with that character throughout the novel. Walter Morel has come home drunk. Gertrude has characteristically "stiffened herself" and pronounced judgment on him with the phrase "The house is filthy with you." Morel, his face suddenly "red" with uncontrollable fury, tells her to get out of his house ("It's me as brings th' money whoam," he cruelly reminds her) and pushes her out the door when she declines to go, "slotting the bolt behind her with a bang." Then he goes back into the kitchen, "drop[s] into his arm-chair, his head, bursting full of blood, sinking between his knees." He falls into "a stupor, from exhaustion and intoxication" (22–23).

Whereas Morel is associated with filth, stupor, heat, and the color red, Gertrude is ultimately associated, in the paragraphs that follow, with control, consciousness, coolness, and colors suggesting purity. Outside, the "great white light" of a "high and magnificent" moon falls "cold on her" as, for a moment, she stands "helplessly staring at the glistening great rhubarb leaves near the door."

> For a while she could not control her consciousness; mechanically she went over the last scene, then over it again, certain phrases, certain moments coming each time like a brand red-hot down on her soul; and each time she enacted again the past hour, each time

the brand came down at the same points, till the mark was burnt in, and the pain burnt out, and at last she came to herself. (23)

When she comes to herself, she momentarily fears being alone at night, but she triumphs over that fear by "hurr[ying] out of the side garden to the front," where she positions herself in the center of "an immense gulf of white [moon]light." (This bright light is, symbolically, the opposite of the darkness of dark water, that which suggests the unknown, the uncontrollable.) Words, as well as white moonlight, help her once again to gain mental control, this time over her fear of the dark and over her memory of the pain she has just been feeling intensely. (She murmurs "to herself over and over again: 'The nuisance! the nuisance!' " [23]).

Finally, Gertrude becomes so aware, so conscious, of where and who she is, that she senses the presence of "something about her," something that is to help her complete her triumph over the passions of fear and anger and other dark unknowns. "With an effort" she "rouse[s] herself to see what" has "penetrated her consciousness." (Hers is a consciousness that is, in its normal state, itself crystallized, hard, cold, and rigid. Whatever penetrates it must be in some sense akin to it.) What she sees are "tall white lilies." The air is "charged with their perfume, as with a presence."

> She touched the big, pallid flowers on their petals, then shivered. They seemed to be stretching in the moonlight. She put her hand into one white bin: the gold scarcely showed on her fingers by moonlight. She bent down to look at the binful of yellow pollen; but it only appeared dusky. Then she drank a deep draught of the scent. It almost made her dizzy. (23–24)

The experience is as close as Gertrude comes in the book to a sensual experience in nature. The lilies are "big," "stretching," "tall," and thus at least as male as they are female. Although Gertrude is a character who tends to touch with thought alone, she touches these lilies with her fingers. When she drinks a deep draught of the scent of the big white flowers she comes as close as she ever is to getting drunk on anything, to relaxing her consciousness enough to experience ecstasy.

Somehow, though, the flowers that make Gertrude feel dizzy with delight are so much, themselves, associated with a pure, aphysical, even spiritual world that Gertrude's enjoyment of them manages to seem something other than a sensualist's rapture. The white lily is, after all, the Easter flower, symbolizing Christ's transcendence of the imperfect, natural world of pain and death. The lilies contain pollen, but the pollen seems somehow unreal, too good for this world, for it scarcely shows on the fingers, and its golden color is pictured in the light of the imagination: in the bright moonlight it is merely "dusky." Most important, the lilies seem like Gertrude, who is both heavy with child and, at the same time, possessed of something that society iden- tifies as male: the will to stand tall and independent, the drive to rise above conditions. Like Gertrude, the lilies are "reeling," but they are tall, stretching, rising above the low, green world about them, the world typified by the low, "thick thorn hedge," the "clumps of white phlox," and the "moth" that "ricochetted" over those humbler, sim- pler flowers, with their "raw, strong scent" (23, 24).

Thus, although the lilies cause Gertrude to "los[e] herself" for awhile, cause her consciousness to "melt" like "scent," and cause her to "swoon" to the point that "the hills and lilies and houses" all "sw[i]m together," the air in which they cause her to swoon is "shiny, pale." It is a rarefied atmosphere in which they grow, and Gertrude's passionate communion with them is more like the passionate ecstasy of a saint who has found, unexpectedly, a kindred spirit than like the swoon of a sensualist who has sought and found simple, natural pleasure.

Throughout the novel, Lawrence identifies certain characters with colors that reflect their natures, colors that can then be used to hint at the nature of a character who is appearing for the first time—or to hint at the complexity of a character we are just getting to know. (Clara Dawes seems a sensualist, far more like Walter Morel than the puritanical Gertrude. And yet long before we see that she has an intellectual, spiritual side, Lawrence suggests her complexity by associating her with the color white as well as red.) Sometimes Lawrence makes a color stand for a given tendency or quality by repeatedly introducing it in scenes in which those qualities are dominant and effective. Often, though, he aids the reader's understanding by working with colors that already have traditional, conventional associations—as he does when he suggests spirituality or a puritanical temperament with the color white or a passionate nature by the color red.

There are, of course, colors that either have no definite, conventional associations or have different, and even conflicting ones. The color gold, for instance, could suggest materialism; Lawrence often identifies it with spiritualism by making it appear in scenes dominated by characters who seek to lay up immaterial treasures in heaven. (Gertrude's hair "has gold threads in it," according to John Field, when he sees it catching the sunlight for the first time.) Blue is another color that could be used to represent anything from aristocratic background (the phrases "blue-blooded" and "blue stocking" suggest birth and wealth respectively) to virginity. Blue is, after all, the liturgical color of the Virgin Mary, and in passages devoted to Miriam Leivers, the madonnalike, intellectual girl with whom Paul Morel eventually falls in love, blue seems to signify sexual virginity. But long before he introduces Miriam or alludes to her nunlike coldness Lawrence associates the color blue with Gertrude Morel, making it, along with white and gold, one of her "primary" colors. By doing so he has invested it with primary meanings. He has made it stand for a proud but brooding intellect, for self-sacrificial spirituality, and for the fierce consciousness and self-consciousness that prevent enjoyment of the physical side of life.

Gertrude is first associated with the color blue in the scene in which we catch our first glimpse of Paul, the baby boy who is doomed to be much like both his mother and Miriam. When we first see the as-yet-unnamed baby, we see it "restless on his mother's knee," already (like a white lily or his own, dissatisfied mother) "clambering" to reach "the light." Gertrude notices "the peculiar knitting of the baby's brows, and the peculiar heaviness of its eyes, as if it were trying to understand something that was pain." She is not the only one present who sees the baby as "brooding" either. "He looks as if he were thinking about something—quite sorrowful," a neighbor woman remarks:

> Suddenly, looking at him, the heavy feeling at the mother's heart melted into passionate grief. She bowed over him, and a few tears shook swiftly out of her very heart. The baby lifted his fingers.
> "My lamb!" she cried softly. . . .
> The baby was looking up at her. It had blue eyes like her own. . . . Its deep blue eyes, always looking up at her unblinking, seemed to draw her innermost thoughts out of her. She no longer loved her husband; she had not wanted this child to come, and there it lay in her arms and pulled at her heart. . . .
> "I will call him Paul," she said suddenly; she knew not why. (36–37)

Paul is, it seems, to be his mother's child; while Gertrude feels guilt in her "soul," the "soul" of the baby, too, seems "burdened," even "stunned." Moreover, Paul is, like his mother, associated with intellect as well as soul. (He seems to be "brooding," "thinking," attempting to "understand" that which is strange and therefore frightening to him.) This soulful, spiritual "lamb" not only seems preternaturally thoughtful from birth but draws "the innermost thoughts" out of "his mother."

Gertrude is, of course, projecting some thoughts onto her helpless baby, only to draw them out again. And Paul, as Lawrence later shows, is not entirely like his mother. (He is black as well as blue, red as well as white.) But much of what Gertrude sees in her infant's eyes and face really is there. Lawrence lets us know that it is by having the neighbor woman Mrs. Kirk independently notice and comment upon the thoughtful, sorrowful nature of the child. More important, he uses the color blue to suggest that mother and baby mirror one another at those two outward, visible points at which the inner intelligence and soul seem nearest to the surface. The mutually reflexive pairs of eyes give credibility to Gertrude's sense that her thoughts are mirrored in— and mirroring—those burdening her infant's young mind.

Lawrence reconfirms our sense that Paul shares his mother's brooding, thoughtful, spiritual nature by mirroring the early scene in which the color blue is introduced in a later one. The later scene, to be sure, reverses the positions of mother and son; nonetheless, it makes exactly the same point: Paul is, like his mother, deeply and consciously thoughtful and spiritual. In the later scene, found in the chapter describing the protagonist's "Young Life," Paul is once again lying down, this time on a sofa near where his mother is ironing clothes. In his "semi-conscious sleep," the boy is vaguely aware of "the clatter of the iron on the iron-stand, of the faint thud, thud on the ironing-board."

> Once roused, he opened his eyes to see his mother standing on the hearth-rug with the hot iron near her cheek, listening, as it were, to the heat. Her still face, with the mouth closed tight from suffering and disillusion and self-denial, and her nose the smallest bit on one side, and her blue eyes so young, quick, and warm, made his heart contract with love. (66)

This time it is the son interpreting his mother's face as being thoughtful and worried. It is Paul, not Gertrude, who is simultaneously struck with his mother's brooding, sensitive, soulful nature—and, simultaneously, with her "quick" blue eyes. Paul does not call his mother "lamb," for it is not a son's place to see a mother as being Christ-like in self-sacrifice. (It is, rather, a mother's place to live the martyr's life vicariously, through the life of a sensitive, intelligent, spiritual son.) But his heart does contract with love, just as hers had some ten years earlier.

Lawrence gives form to *Sons and Lovers* by pairing and opposing characters, characters who are associated with traits and with sets of colors and other signifiers ("cold," "hard," "rigid," "proud," "intellectual," "independent," "conscious") that call those traits to mind. Gertrude Morel— who is to a great, even tragic, extent like her son Paul— is to a great and tragic extent the opposite of her husband, Morel.

"She herself was opposite" her "soft, non-intellectual, warm" husband, Lawrence says at one point. Five pages later he says that "he was too different from her," and, two pages further on, in "The Early Life of the Morels," we again learn: "The pity was, she was too much his opposite. She could not be content with the little he might be; she would have him the much that he ought to be. So, in seeking to make him nobler than he could be, she destroyed him" (9, 14, 16).

We can see in the latter passage, once again, Gertrude's intellectual and moral instincts. She evaluates and judges life constantly. She assesses her own position in it, notes the defects of the world around her, and comes to conclusions about the way things could be, if only others were "nobler" and trying harder, as they "ought to be." We see also, once again, her fierce pride, will, and ambition, characteristics that will not let her—even in the face of evidence that she should—abandon the dream of a finer, better life. An earlier passage has shown us that her husband, whom she met at a Christmas party when she was twenty-three, shares none of the qualities that make his wife her father's daughter. Lawrence characterizes Walter through words such as *soft, warm, wavy, moist, rich, pleasant, comic, ready*, and—perhaps most important—*non-intellectual*. For Morel is a physical man, relatively unconscious and unselfconscious, that is to say, undominated by and even unaware of the mental side of life that *is* life to his wife, Gertrude.

> He had wavy black hair that shone . . . and a vigorous black beard that had never been shaved. His cheeks were ruddy, and his red, moist mouth was noticeable because he laughed so often and so heartily. He had that rare thing, a rich, ringing laugh. Gertrude Coppard had watched him, fascinated. He was so full of colour and animation, his voice ran so easily into comic grotesque, he was so ready and so pleasant with everybody. Her own father had a rich fund of humour, but it was satiric. This man's was different: soft, non-intellectual, warm, a kind of gambolling. (9)

The contrast between Walter's sense of humor and Gertrude's father's sense of humor is telling—and all the more so because we know how similar Gertrude's character or nature is to that of her father. Satire is intellectual humor, a humor born of a cold, critical outlook on life and of the desire to teach a lesson, to make people more conscious of shortcomings and needs for improvement. Satire employs irony, which Lawrence identifies with Saint Paul, who was harsh in government and unsympathetic by nature. "Gambolling," on the other hand, means "frisking" or "frolicking" or even "dancing" humor. "Gambolling" humor suggests a humor that is physical and entertaining—in the way of slapstick comedy—not intellectual and critical like satire.

Whereas Lawrence associates Gertrude Morel with colors such as white, gold, and blue, he associates her husband with red and black. ("He had wavy black hair" and a "vigorous black beard"; "his cheeks were ruddy," his "red moist mouth . . . noticeable.") But, because Lawrence is an artist who creates structures only to complicate them, thereby making the reader think, he also associates Walter with the word "gold." He allows the reader to distinguish between his two usages by associating Walter with a "gold" that seems dusky and dark, not bright and yellow; soft and even liquid, not hard and metallic: "She was puritan, like her father, high-minded, and really stern. Therefore the dusky, golden softness of this man's sensuous flame of life, that flowed off his flesh like the flame from a candle, not baffled and gripped into incandescence by thought and spirit as her life was, seemed to her something wonderful, beyond her" (10).

Two entirely different things can be signified by the word *humour*: intellectual satire and crude but delightful slapstick. Words help us to understand, and yet we have to be wary of them. *Gold,* like *humour,* is a term that helps us to understand only if we understand that, like all words, it can be used to describe both one thing or person and another entirely different thing or person, in this case a person mysterious to, utterly "beyond" the other. As we come to understand the different uses of words, we not only become sensitive to the complexity of the text but also to the complexity of human nature: for that is what *Sons and Lovers* is, finally, about. What is this thing called human nature that is so complicated and contradicted that we almost seem to need two different languages to describe it—a metaphor using *gold* to suggest Gertrude's spiritualism and another using the same term to signify the warm, rich sensuality of Walter? We seem to need one *black* to signify the physical, instinctual, amoral life of a coal miner, and another to suggest the harsh, colorless sternness of his wife Gertrude, who is associated with the purity of white but also pictured, throughout the novel, dressed in puritan black. And how can terms like *ruddy* and *red* and, especially, *inflamed* symbolize passion when there are so many, contradictory passions , i.e., sexual passion but also the angry passion that "inflame[s]" Gertrude's "soul" when her husband locks her out of the house?

Unless we are trained to the subtleties of human nature, we will see Gertrude only as a woman and not recognize the subtle, hidden, but extreme differences between Gertrude and other women, differences that make her unhappy with both her world and herself. Unless we are trained to the subtleties of human nature, we will see Morel as a man's man, and miss the fact that the word *man* can be as misleading a term to describe him as the word *humorous* can be to describe Gertrude's father. Morel "was well set-up, erect, and very smart," but he is also "non-intellectual" and "soft," not "gripped" as his wife is said to be, and therefore not "erect" in the way that she is when she "pursue[s]" the timid John Field. She is the one who has "grit"; it is she, not he, who is "hard as rock."

It is he, not she, on the other hand, who is naturally good at listening, the thing his wife must do as a woman. He can comfortably listen, moreover, because he is not prone to analyze and criticize the things he hears. "She saw him listen deferentially," Lawrence says in a sentence that allows us to see Walter through the filter of Gertrude's always-assessing mind, "but without understanding" (11). Because he either cannot or will not understand everything that happens about him, he is unhindered in life by the kind of obsessive carefulness that characterizes his wife. "He risk[s] his life daily, and with gaiety," and he is as careless with his words as he is with his body. "[H]e could only abuse the pit managers. He would say, in the Palmerston [tavern]: 'Th' gaffer come down to our stall this morning, an' 'e says, "You know, Walter, this 'ere'll not do. What about these props?" An' I says to him, "Why, what art talkin' about? What d'st mean about th' props?" "It'll never do, this 'ere," 'e says. "You'll be havin' th' roof in, one o' these days." An' I says, "Tha'd better stan' on a bit o' clunch, then, an' hold it up wi' thy 'ead." So 'e wor that mad, 'e cossed an' 'e swore an t'other chaps they did laugh.' " (16–17). Walter talks loosely and openly because "Authority" is "hateful to him," because he resents the fact that others would like to impose controls on a life that he himself has no interest in controlling. Unlike Gertrude and unlike most other men, who must have everything outside and inside them under control, Walter lives by anarchic principles, if by any at all. He even "loathed a fork," preferring to eat his food with a "clasp-knife," alone, with "the blinds down and the candle lit even when it was daylight" (27).

To some extent, Lawrence admits, Walter's characteristics have been learned. The fork, after all, is a "modern introduction which has still scarcely reached common people." As for Morel's habit of eating alone in the dark, even during the daylight hours, "it was the habit of the mine," where there is never any light. Still, Walter is by nature antimodern, almost primitive, a creature of darkness and of the instincts, not of thought and morality and civilized regimen. Even in the mines, where the failure to be aware of the work environment can cause injury and even death, Morel is a carefree loner, a man of frenzy, sweat, even savagery. Lawrence pictures him, one day, at quitting time:

> "Hey-up there—*loose-a*'!" cried the men, leaving the next stall.
> Morel continued to strike.
> "Tha'll happen catch me up," said Barker, departing.
> When he had gone, Morel, left alone, felt savage. He had not finished his job. He had overworked himself into a frenzy. Rising, wet with sweat, he threw his stool down, pulled on his coat, blew out his candle, took his lamp, and went. (30)

Morel would rather work on alone than quit, not because he is a man possessed by the bourgeois ethic that drove his father-in-law, not because he has a proud independent nature like that of his wife, but simply because he has poured himself, physically, into a job that is still unfinished. He can no more think in terms of a whistle or punch clock than he can eat food properly with a fork. Thus, although he can be a hard worker, he is not a good worker in the modern, industrial sense. He does not know when to begin or quit working, playing, drinking. At work, as at play, he lives a life of wild, loose, frenzied *un*control. Men who arrive and leave work on time, who do things carefully and by the book, are more appreciated and better rewarded.

They are also less likely to be ill or injured, for the careless gaiety with which Walter Morel lives life is dangerous below ground. When Walter is seriously injured, moreover, he might as well be in hell, for the hospital is a place where sweat, savagery, frenzy, and reckless freedom have no place. "[F]or a man like your father," Mrs. Morel tells her son, Paul, "the hospital *is* hard. He *can't* understand rules and regulations. And he won't let anybody else touch him, not if he can help it. When he smashed the muscles of his thigh, and it had to be dressed four times a day, *would* he let anybody but me or his mother do it? He wouldn't" (87).

Like his portrait of Gertrude, Lawrence's portrait of Walter Morel is both sympathetic and unsympathetic. He is, certainly, critical of Morel's uncivilized, savage energy when it is directed at the physically helpless Gertrude. As a child, Lawrence lay in bed more than once and listened to the horrible sounds of his drunken father physically abusing his proud and moral Christian mother. He records one of those sleepless nights in "Discord in Childhood," a poem published in *Amores* in 1916. "Outside the house," the poet writes, ". . . when the wind rose," the "terrible whips" of an "ash-tree . . . / Shrieked and slashed the wind. . . ."

> Within the house two voices arose, a slender lash
> Whistling she-delirious rage, and the dreadful sound
> Of a male thong booming and bruising, until it had drowned
> The other voice in a silence of blood, 'neath the noise of the ash.[54]

In *Sons and Lovers*, Lawrence pictures Paul in bed listening silently, invisibly, to the same horrible sounds.

Opposition and Conflict

In front of the house was a huge old ash-tree. . . . [T]error came in from the shrieking of the tree and the anguish of the home discord. Often Paul would wake up . . . aware of thuds downstairs. Instantly he was wide awake. Then he heard the booming shouts of his father . . . then the sharp replies of his mother. . . . And then the whole was drowned in a piercing medley of shrieks and cries from the great, wind-swept ash-tree. . . . There was a feeling of horror, a kind of bristling in the darkness, and a sense of blood. (59–60)

But there are scenes, too, that testify to a better side of Walter Morel, to the fact that all facets of human character have a positive as well as a negative impact upon the world. For instance, one of the positive by-products of the miner's naturalness, instinctiveness, and freedom from both external authority and the internal authorities we call conscience and self-consciousness is creativity. Lawrence pictures him, in chapter 4, singing while at work cobbling boots and mending the kettle.

Then he always wanted several attendants, and the children enjoyed it. They united with him in the work. . . . It was nice to see him run with a piece of red-hot iron into the scullery, crying:
"Out of my road—out of my road!"
Then he hammered the soft, red glowing stuff on his iron goose, and made the shape he wanted. Or he sat absorbed for a moment, soldering. Then the children watched with joy as the metal sank suddenly molten, and was shoved about against the nose of the soldering-iron, while the room was full of a scent of burnt resin and hot tin, and Morel was silent and intent for a minute. He always sang when he mended boots because of the jolly sound of hammering. (63)

Once again, Morel is associated with the colors red and black. Once again, he is associated with the world underground. (The references to burning resin and hot metal make Morel's workroom seem something like a devil's workshop.) Nevertheless, *Sons and Lovers* is the story of a young painter's development; as such it might have been given the title that Joyce was to give his autobiographical novel three years later: *A Portrait of the Artist as a Young Man*. It is clear that

Paul cannot hate everything his father is and does without hating part of himself. Indeed, Paul might have been a better artist had he been born with a little more of his father's iconoclastic creativity and anarchic freedom, for the younger man's art is usually described by Lawrence as being "clever," that is to say, intellectual. Paul's creative energies, inherited from his father, are strained and filtered through a consciousness and self-consciousness inherited from his mother. Form may be gained in the process of exerting control over the medium; Walter's iron works are, after all, most beautiful when they are still in molten, fluid, unfixed form. But a bit more fluidity and naturalness, a little less tightness and self-consciousness, would have helped, not hindered, Paul's artistic production.

It is tempting to oversimplify things, to say that, through the characters of Walter and Gertrude Morel, Lawrence is generalizing about the males and females of the human species, associating asexuality, spirituality, softness, purity, receptivity, and long-suffering tolerance with femininity while aligning physicality, instinct, sweat, drunkenness, meanness, and even violence, with masculinity. But, as we have begun to see, Lawrence is doing something far different. For to suggest that men are hard and physical, women soft and spiritual, is to confirm old stereotypes, whereas what Lawrence more nearly does in *Sons and Lovers* is to throw into question the old assumptions about gender. He shows us that it is in Gertrude's nature to be those things that his society expects men to be: proud, ambitious, concerned with money, defiant, intellectual, stern, rigid, even hard as a rock. And Walter, the man "she tried to force . . . constantly" (14), is many of those things Lawrence's society expected women to be: soft, nonintellectual, warm, sensuous, deferential, nonunderstanding, and even afraid. He does, to be sure, risk his life daily with gaiety in the mine, but when it comes to dealing with people psychologically and with words, he cannot "pursue" the way his wife can. Gertrude bombards him with questions so rhetorical that Lawrence does not even end them with question marks, and Walter absorbs the verbal projectiles—that is, up to the point at which he feels the urge to fight back physically.

"Ah, wouldn't I, wouldn't I have gone long ago, but for those children. Ay, haven't I repented not going years ago, when I'd only the one"—suddenly drying into rage. "Do you think it's for *you* I stop—do you think I'd stop one minute for *you*?"

"Go then," he shouted, beside himself. "Go!"

"No!" She faced round. "No," she cried loudly, "you shan't have it *all* your own way; you shan't do *all* you like. I've got those children to see to. My word," she laughed, "I should look well to leave them to you."

"Go," he cried thickly, lifting his fist. He was afraid of her. "Go!" (22–23)

The word *go* is one of only two words Walter can say in response to Gertrude's pointed rhetorical attack, and even that word he says "thickly." "My word," Gertrude says back at one point, and although she means only to use a common, idiomatic expression, the "word" is, indeed, hers. And he is "afraid" of her and her word.

Fear is one of the attributes besides nonintellectualism and sensual softness that make Walter something other than the stereotypical male. There are, of course, still other attributes. Although Walter is nonverbal in the sense that he is nonargumentative, he is verbal in the way society expects women to be verbal. Unlike his wife, he is a gossip: "He was blab-mouthed, a tongue-wagger" (16). He is also, as we can see in the passage in which he recounts his exchange with the pit manager, "a good mimic" (17). (The fact that he enjoys mimicking people suggests Walter's natural tendency to play yet another role that society wants to define as female, for "imitation," like gossip, is secondary speech. That is to say, to imitate is to speak while keeping one's own identity reserved; to gossip is to make or pass along statements behind the scenes rather than openly and publicly, as men are allowed and therefore expected to do.) Furthermore, this man who works on bravely when alone in the coal mines is a whiner above ground. "She hated her husband," Lawrence says at one point, "because, whenever he had an audience, he whined and played for sympathy." Even his little boy, William, who is "sitting nursing the baby [Paul], hated him, *with a boy's* hatred for false sentiment" (35, italics mine).

But a "boy's hatred for false sentiment," Lawrence would have us see, is not naturally associated with maleness. Boys are not born with a hatred for false sentiment, girls with a tendency toward false sentiment. Boys and girls are not naturally predisposed, in other words, to be opposite and at war with one another. Rather, "a boy's hatred for false sentiment," like a girl's proclivity to softness and receptivity, is a behavior trait taught by society. Such traits are, furthermore, traits that some "boys" and "girls" already possess naturally, but that others will find unnatural and, therefore, difficult to adopt. When the latter boys and girls, men and women, try to be—or appear to be—what they are not, they enter into a destructive conflict with their hidden or repressed, true natures that leads them, before long, to destroy others as well as themselves. Mr. Morel's inability to make money and argue intellectually with an ambitious, intellectual, and verbal wife so frustrates him that he beats her viciously. Mrs. Morel's inability to happily adopt a quiet, sensual, receptive identity causes her to hate her husband and, more tragically, to try and accomplish her "male" goals through her sons, who are, themselves, at war with their own inner natures.

5

STRIFE IN LOVE
AND STRIFE WITHIN
Walter, Gertrude, Paul, and Miriam

Many of the events and attitudes portrayed in *Sons and Lovers* are the result of the conflict between a husband and wife, Walter and Gertrude Morel. Many novels published before Lawrence's day, of course, had contained plots driven by such a conflict. Lawrence, however, does more than describe a Nottinghamshire version of the age-old war between the sexes. He shows us the inner frustrations that result when there is a gap between what a man is expected to be and what he is, between what a woman "should" do and what she wants to do deep down. He suggests that the conflict between male and female, husband and wife, is exacerbated by—and may even be caused by—this kind of discord between self and society.

Lawrence is not the first novelist to have written about men and women struggling with wives or lovers on the one hand and with social conventions or expectations on the other. Emily Brontë, George Eliot, and Thomas Hardy had all written novels about women torn between being themselves and being what women were expected to be. All three writers wrote books—such as Hardy's *Far from the Madding Crowd*—in which romantic and marital discord resulted from frustrations caused by society's expectations, definitions, and limitations.

There is one way, however, in which Lawrence goes beyond Brontë, Eliot, Hardy and other great Victorian predecessors. He suggests that every self, be it male or female, is in actuality two selves. Thus the woman who is naturally the way society expects men to be is, at the same time, the way society expects women to be. She is, in other words, conflicted without and within—with the society that expects her to be "female" and with that less assertive side of herself that is what society would call feminine.

A further examination of Gertrude and Walter Morel yields numerous examples of this complicating self-division. Something in Gertrude "hated her father's overbearing manner towards her gentle, humorous, kindly-souled mother," even though Gertrude herself is "overbearing" like her father. In general, "she favoured her mother" physically and her father temperamentally, but not entirely. She has, for instance, her father's blue eyes combined with a face otherwise more like her mother's. And she has a gentle, submissive side to her nature that, though usually subordinate to her dominant, domineering side, causes her to "hate" that aspect of her father that is, unfortunately, her own dominant aspect (7). Thus, loathing of the father is evidence of self-loathing, which in turn implies a duplicity of the inner character itself.

There is another way in which Gertrude is doubled within. She is capable of being "puritan" and yet, at the same time, sensual. Sometimes, for instance, she thinks that her husband's golden softness is "fascinat[ing]," even "wonderful" (9, 10). Lawrence is not merely suggesting that opposites are attracted to one another; he is suggesting, rather, that if they are, it is because each human self contains, within it, opposite selves. Thus, a puritanical temperament may dominate a self that contains, nonetheless, a sensual, loose, amoral side as well. That sensual self, though seldom publicly expressed, can be attracted to the sensuality and amorality that is outwardly expressed by another person.

As we saw in the last chapter, the white and gold lily in the garden that Gertrude communes with after being locked out of the house suggests purity and the will to transcend the lowness, the ugliness of life. It is thus, to some extent, like Gertrude, and it is even associated with the resurrected Christ. Still, Gertrude communes with it sensually, not intellectually, which suggests that she has a dark sensual side as well as a bright, spiritual or intellectual one. Indeed, Lawrence subtly suggests that the lily, in spite of its white radiant aspect in "an immense gulf of white light" (23), may remind Gertrude of Walter subconsciously, the man who has just treated her so shamelessly. When she touches the "big pallid flowers" of "the tall white lilies," she seems almost to be touching her husband sexually, for cupped inside those flowers is a "dusky"–colored "gold" that "scarcely showed . . . by moonlight" (24). Only a few pages earlier, Lawrence has spoken of "the dusky, golden softness of [Walter's] sensuous flame of life" (10). Gertrude may not drink liquor, but she does, while lovingly handling these flowers that are much like her sensual husband, drink in the scented air until "it almost made her dizzy." Consequently, "the hills and lilies and houses, all swum together in a kind of swoon" (24).

Again and again, Lawrence shows us just a glimpse of Gertrude's sensuous, physical nature in scenes in which it is her opposed, spiritual or intellectual nature that is dominant and most in evidence. Certainly, Gertrude spends afternoons discussing sermons with the young Mr. Heaton because she longs for elevated discourse, and yet when she is with Heaton, there is something inside her that wants to bring this proponent of pure, spiritual love down gently "to earth."

> "When He changed the water into wine at Cana," he said, "that is a symbol that the ordinary life, even the blood, of the married husband and wife, which had before been uninspired, like water, became filled with the Spirit, and was as wine, because, when love enters, the whole spiritual constitution of a man changes, is filled with the Holy Ghost, and almost his form is altered."
>
> Mrs. Morel thought to herself:
>
> "Yes, poor fellow, his young wife is dead; that is why he makes his love into the Holy Ghost." (33)

To some extent, of course, it is a bad marriage that makes Gertrude respond cynically to the young minister's reverie. To some extent, however, Gertrude responds in the way she does because she knows that love between husband and wife is—must be—made with the body.

Because there is a side of Mrs. Morel's nature that is much like the dominant, sensual side of her husband, her relationship with her husband is necessarily a love-hate relationship. Part of Gertrude wants Walter dead while the other part wants to make love to him. "Now he fell seriously ill," Lawrence says at the beginning of chapter 3, "and Mrs. Morel had him to nurse. He was one of the worst patients imaginable. But, in spite of all, and putting aside the fact that he was the breadwinner, she never quite wanted him to die. Still there was one part of her wanted him for herself" (45).

The man that Gertrude Morel simultaneously wishes would die and wants for herself is similarly self-divided, though to a lesser degree. Somewhere inside Morel there is a moral, spiritual nature (his very name suggests the possibility), a will to consciousness and conscience that makes for fear of the night and preference for light. We are most often allowed glimpses of that recessive side of Walter's character toward the ends of scenes in which husband and wife have been fighting. "Open the door, Walter," Gertrude says coldly after she has awakened from her uncharacteristically sensual communion with the lilies and the night air. "His hands relaxed. It dawned on him what he had done. His head dropped, sullen and dogged. She saw him hurry to the door, heard the bolt chock." Suddenly, Lawrence presents the picture not from the perspective of Gertrude, who is outside looking in, but rather from her husband's interior vantage point:

> He tried the latch. It opened—and there stood the silver-grey night, fearful to him, after the tawny light of the lamp. He hurried back.
>   When Mrs. Morel entered, she saw him almost running through the door to the stairs. He had ripped his collar off his neck in his haste to be gone ere she came in, and there it lay with bursten button-holes. It made her angry. (25–26)

Lawrence specifically tells us that Walter "had not a grain of physical fear," that if she "had been twenty burglars, he would have gone blindly for them" (25). Is he, then, only afraid of angry words? Certainly, he has been known to be afraid of his wife's words, but here he is afraid of something more terrible than any verbal barrage that could possibly ensue. He first feels afraid when he sees the darkness of the night while "st[anding]" at the open door. Darkness is used by Lawrence throughout the novel to represent Walter's subterranean, instinctual, sensual, and unconscious nature. He is said to be afraid of the dark, moreover, because he has been in a lamp's "tawny light," which we may take to represent a consciousness and self-consciousness not usually associated with the drunken miner who loves to dance but is "without understanding." Consciousness of "what he had done" has made Morel run from Gertrude but also from himself. The very ability to become conscious of what he has done—to feel guilty about it— shows that Morel has two sides, not one, and justifies those occasional, surprising inconsistencies of color and symbol that Lawrence uses to represent him. Hard as it may be to believe, the fact is that Morel is capable of feeling guilt in the way that a more "puritanical" person feels it, and because of this, he is capable not only of fearing the night but also of being associated with a tawny lamp and even with the light of dawn. "It dawned on him what he had done" is, after all, the way Lawrence chooses to describe the moment in which his most unconscious character comes to consciousness.

In the first few pages of *Sons and Lovers,* Lawrence says that Walter "was too different from" Gertrude, which presumably implies that husband and wife are not perfect opposites. Then, in the very next sentence, he says that "his nature was purely sensuous." If the two are not perfect opposites—"too different," but not entirely different—that means either that Gertrude is not "purely" asensual or that Lawrence has exaggerated the case somewhat in saying that Walter is exclusively sensual. The more we read of *Sons and Lovers,* the more it seems that Gertrude is partly Walter-like, and Walter, though he is less self-contradicted and therefore less capable of self-hatred than any other major character in the novel, is not "purely" one thing or the other. For instance, the scene in which Morel fights with his wife, lets her back into the house, and then runs to hide is not the only one in which Morel exhibits a sense of guilt that attests to the presence of another self or, at least, a self composed of contradictory sides. After the very next fight, a horrible conflict that ends when he smashes her head with the corner of a silverware drawer that he has jerked out of its cabinet frame, we once again see that Walter contains a sliver of that "consciousness" that almost purely defines his wife's makeup. Mentally, the morning after the battle, "He tried to wriggle out of it. 'It was her own fault,' he said to himself. Nothing, however, could prevent his inner consciousness inflicting on him the punishment which ate into his spirit like rust, and which he could only alleviate by drinking" (41). It is usually Gertrude, not Morel, who "[cannot] control her consciousness," who "mechanically" goes over "the last scene" feeling the "redhot . . . brand" of mental pain (23). This time it is Morel who is mentally branding himself, and although his behavior has been criminal, Lawrence seems to disapprove of a punishing inner consciousness, which eats into the spirit like rust, almost as much as he does of the violence that produced the guilt in the first place. This seems shocking until we realize that Lawrence is subtly analyzing an unbroken chain of violence against self and others that results when society cannot tolerate two kinds of men and women, when men and women cannot accept their own double, contradictory natures. Morel is unhappy with the role that society expects him to play because he is a man, so he drinks. Once drunk, he makes a victim of his wife, who is already the victim not only of a role that society expects her to play but also of her own double nature, which wants to be a puritanical intellect but also a sensuous lover. Having beaten his wife, Morel suddenly feels the upsurge of his "other" nature, that "consciousness" that causes him to hate his dominant, "savage" or "frenzied" self. The self-conflict sends him back to the bottle, which in turn allows the kind of conflict that eventually brings out the "brand" or "rust" of consciousness again.

Thus, *Sons and Lovers* is a novel of conflict—of strife within as well as between selves. We have begun this discussion of Lawrence's work by considering the battles that are waged within and between Mr. and Mrs. Morel; those conflicts, after all, to a great extent determine the second generation conflicts, namely, those within and between their children and other younger characters. One of these second generation characters is, of course, Paul, the protagonist of *Sons and Lovers*. His inner and outer conflicts are central to the novel's plot, and yet they are best understood as the products of wars waged between—and in—the bodies and souls of his parents.

It is apparent, then, that *Sons and Lovers* has a definite form, pattern, or structure, even though it closely parallels the story of the young D. H. Lawrence. Lawrence has formed this novel, which has often been interpreted as if it were autobiography, around pairs of characters. Sometimes like characters are paired; just as often, however, Lawrence pairs opposites. There are, too, pairs of characters who are deeply self-divided; often members of such a pair complement each other, one individual being slightly more physical than spiritual, more instinctual than intellectual, the counterpart character being ruled—but barely—by his or her mental and spiritual yearnings.

Walter and Gertrude Morel are almost always paired as opposites. But together they form only one of many sets of characters who are yoked together by conflict. Indeed, the conflict between Mr. and Mrs. Morel, husband and wife, is mirrored by the father-son conflict that goes on between Mr. Morel and Paul, who, in turn, is paired with his mother in likeness. Critics have often returned to the subject of Paul's love for his mother, discussing it in both biographical and Freudian terms, that is to say, as a reflection of Lawrence's Oedipal affection for his own mother. They have consequently assumed that Paul's hostile relationship to his father is founded in jealousy, for in the Oedipal situation, father and son are, inevitably, rivals.

It is not necessary, however, to understand the bond between Paul and his mother in either biographical or Freudian terms. Neither do we need, necessarily, to understand the conflict between Paul and his father as a conflict grounded in sexual jealousies generated between D. H. Lawrence and his father by a Freudian "family romance" that Lawrence and his mother were involved in. For instance, we can understand the attraction between Gertrude and Paul, the hostility between Gertrude and Walter, and the hostility between Walter and Paul as a set of destructively intense alliances and conflicts produced by a society that narrowly defines the roles that men and women may properly play. A proud willful woman who cannot satisfy her own ambitious nature directly—because women are given no public outlet for ambition or will—is likely to come to resent a husband through whom she cannot indirectly reach her high goal. If she has a son who is more like herself—and more like what a man in a given society is expected to be—she may form too close a bond with that son through whom she can achieve vicariously.

What, then, happens to a soft, receptive, musical, and humorous father who cannot be appreciated—or fully appreciated—by his wife? He is likely to come to resent not only the son whose talents are more properly "male" but also his wife, who comes to appreciate her son more than she does her husband in spite of those natural, untaught instincts that initially drew her toward the man she married. If resentment leads a husband to hurt his wife, then the son through whom she is living her life is bound to protect the mother he so resembles.

Thus, the powerful attractions and repulsions that lock Walter, Gertrude, and Paul in love and conflict may be understood in light of socially induced frustrations and needs, which do, of course, have psychological and sexual repercussions. The bonds and tensions within the Morel family can, moreover, be understood in aesthetic terms, that is to say, as a set of formally arranged forces of attraction and repulsion that define the spaces between characters in Lawrence's novel. In other words, rather than first looking at love and hate and deep ambivalence in the novel through the lens of Freudian theory, we may look at them as evidence of polarities that Lawrence sets up between and within characters in a work of art. These polarities give the novel that beauty that resides in perceptible form or symmetry. The form or symmetry established between Gertrude, Walter, and Paul extends outward to encompass all the novel's major characters. Paul and his mother, for instance, are fundamentally similar to another person whose story is told by the novel: Miriam Leivers. A second three-way relationship, this one involving Paul and Gertrude and Miriam, is grounded in—and evidence of—that likeness. But because Paul is unlike Miriam in a few important ways, conflicts develop, conflicts not unlike the ones between Paul's father and mother.

The remainder of this chapter will examine the ways in which Paul is paired with his mother. Paul is, of course, not entirely like the predominantly spiritual, intellectual, and "conscious" Gertrude; he has more than a little of his physical, instinctual, "unconscious" father in him. But Gertrude's dominant characteristics do predominate, and therefore Paul and his mother are united in and by a similar conflict with the father. It may be helpful to think, both of that unity and of that struggle, in terms of a triangle.

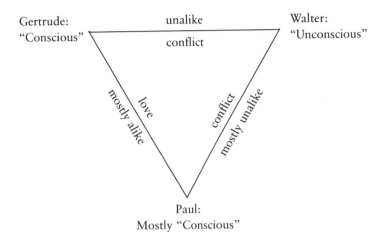

Gertrude: "Conscious" unalike / conflict Walter: "Unconscious"

mostly alike / love conflict / mostly unalike

Paul: Mostly "Conscious"

Let us add Miriam Leivers to the discussion. Miriam, Lawrence shows us, is predominantly like Gertrude Morel, for she is as over-balanced by consciousness as Paul's mother is. Because Paul, too, favors his mother, Miriam is also like Paul. Nevertheless, because the father in Paul is barely and not always repressed or recessive, Miriam is part of a highly complex network.

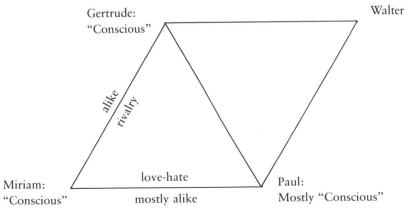

Gertrude: "Conscious" Walter

alike / rivalry

Miriam: "Conscious" love-hate / mostly alike Paul: Mostly "Conscious"

The complexity of this triangle resides in the fact that whereas Miriam is like Gertrude, and less like Paul, she and Gertrude are rivals: thus their very likeness breeds quiet conflict. They are rivals because the spiritual, intellectual, "conscious" side of Paul expresses love for both of them. But because Paul has a darker side, the love he feels—especially for Miriam—is a complex love alternating with hate.

From the novel's second chapter on, Lawrence makes it clear that Paul and his mother are a great deal alike. Certainly, Gertrude is more like Paul than she is like any of her other children: "William grew bigger and strong_. and more active," Lawrence writes in chapter 3, "while Paul, always rather delicate and quiet, got slimmer, and trotted after his mother like her shadow" (48). Earlier in the novel we are told that Paul's blue eyes are exactly "like her own"; now the whole body of the boy seems a reflection or refraction of his mother's.

The image of Paul as his mother's shadow, moreover, is one that Lawrence revises slightly on the same page in order to suggest that Paul's pain is inevitably his mother's pain as well, that she is no more able to separate her condition from her son's than a human body is able to divide itself from its shadow on a sunny day. "These fits were not often," Lawrence says of the times when Paul cried himself to sleep after periods of depression not unlike his mother's, "but they caused a shadow in Mrs. Morel's heart, and her treatment of Paul was different from that of the other children" (48).

The love Paul feels for the mother whose identity he sometimes reflects, sometimes shadows, is counterpointed in the novel by his hatred of the father whom he is so little like. "All the children, but particularly Paul, were peculiarly *against* their father, along with their mother," Lawrence says, adding later in the same chapter that "Paul hated his father."

> As a boy he had a fervent private religion.
> "Make him stop drinking," he prayed every night. "Lord, let my father die," he prayed very often. "Let him not be killed at pit," he prayed when, after tea, his father did not come home from work. (60)

Like all characters in the novel, Paul is a bundle of opposed, conflicting motives, wills, and identities. Just as "part of [Gertrude] wanted" Morel even as part of her "wanted him to die," so part of Paul would rather his father reform and live while another part simply wants him to die.

Although Paul is pulled in several directions at once, he is also, like his mother, dominated by a nature that is at once spiritual and intellectual, and too much of both to allow him to sympathize much or often with his earthy, physical father. Although born too late to accept fully the tenets of the religion his mother practices puritanically, Paul is nonetheless religious by nature. (It is significant that he couches even his wish that his father would die in terms of "a fervent private religion.") Paul is not only the "shadow" of his mother in the sense that he is so like her as to seem her alter ego or double; he is also her shadow in the sense that, like her, he is aphysical—mostly "shade," a word that in Lawrence's day suggested ghost, soul, and spirit. It is "peace of soul" that Paul seeks by sleeping with his mother, not the bodily peace that follows physical lovemaking. And he finds it with her because she, like her son, is soulful, spiritual, and religious by nature. "Paul lay against her and slept," Lawrence says; "she . . . fell later on into a profound sleep that *seemed to give her faith*" (67, italics mine).

Of course, no one is entirely aphysical, but Lawrence suggests the fact that Paul is more "shade" than substance by describing the boy's body in such a way as to contrast it with a brother's more substantial body on the one hand and to compare it directly with Gertrude's wispy presence on the other. "William grew bigger and stronger and more active," Lawrence writes in a passage that pairs William and Paul as opposites, "while Paul, always rather delicate and quiet, got slimmer" (48). By using the word *delicate* Lawrence strengthens the pairing he has created between Paul and his mother by using the very same word he uses in his first description of Gertrude's physical nature: "she was a delicate, rather proud child" (7).

Just as Gertrude was a "proud child," one who enjoyed being petted by the men at the dockyard more because it fed her considerable sense of self-importance than because of the physical pleasure of being petted, so Paul, too, is proud and willful. We are made aware of that pride in scenes like the one in which he goes out to pick mushrooms and blueberries and stays out "all day," trudging "miles and miles, rather than own himself beaten and come home to [his mother] empty-handed" (68). His pride, like his mother's, moreover, exists alongside a high degree of consciousness or sensitivity. When he goes to the mining offices to pick up his father's paycheck, he is asked, ribbingly, what they teach at "Board-school" (73). Paul is infuriated to a degree that both recalls and revives his mother's youthful hatred of any and all demeaning situations. "[S]ometimes the fury in his eyes roused her, made her sleeping soul lift up its head a moment, surprised," Lawrence says just after telling us that "his ridiculous hypersensitiveness made her heart ache" (73). The effect of the juxtaposition is clear: Gertrude's heart aches with understanding of what it feels like to be as ridiculously proud, even haughty, and therefore as absurdly conscious of status—and of slights—as she herself has long been.

Thus, whereas Paul's father has been described as "reckless," "heedless," "careless," and full of "gaiety" (83), Paul is shown to be, like his mother, hypersensitive, proud, highly self-conscious, and tightly wound. He is so aware of being and doing, so mentally conscious of his very existence, that he is even aware of the potential awareness of others. Lawrence describes that hyper-consciousness by telling of a summer walk Paul takes with his mother: "Mother and son set off together one Tuesday morning. It was August and blazing hot. Paul walked with something screwed up tight inside him. He would have suffered much physical pain rather than this unreasonable suffering at being exposed to strangers, to be accepted or rejected. Yet he chattered away with his mother. . . . She was gay, like a sweetheart" (92). Whereas Walter can be gay even while risking his life, his wife and son can be gay, can "chatter . . . away," only with one another. Painfully conscious, constantly, of the otherness of the world, Paul and his mother can only relax with one person—the only person who seems not a "stranger" but, rather, a shadow of self.

In addition to being aphysical, religious, proud, and sensitive, Paul is, like his mother, a person of words, not things. To be sure, he is less inclined than she to enjoy discussions of Scripture and theology—the times, after all, are changing from late Victorian piety toward modern agnosticism—but that does not mean he does not have his own bible—as well as his own "fervent private religion." Paul's bible is, of course, literature; just as his mother sees the world through the filter of words that have been taught to her in church and Sunday school, so Paul looks out and sees the world through words bequeathed to him by idealistic poets of the romantic and Victorian periods. He sees Connie, at work, as Elaine, the devoted and long-suffering young virgin of Tennyson's *Idylls of the King*. He sees Miriam Leivers, his first love, as Tennyson's "Lady of Shalott," a young maiden in a tower who, like Elaine, falls in love with the unavailable Lancelot and dies of unrequited love for him.

Paul is constantly accusing Miriam of being tight, of always being self-consciously, intellectually amused but never truly, unselfconsciously happy. "Why can't you laugh?" he asks her at one point.

> "You never laugh laughter. You only laugh when something is odd or incongruous, and then it almost seems to hurt you."
>
> She bowed her head as if he were scolding her.
>
> "I wish you could laugh at me just for one minute—just for one minute. I feel as if it would set something free."
>
> "But"—and she looked up at him with eyes frightened and struggling—"I do laugh at you—I *do*."
>
> "Never! There's always a kind of intensity. When you laugh I could always cry; it seems as if it shows up your suffering. Oh, you make me knit the brows of my very soul and cogitate." (188)

Paul's accusations are hardly fair. The very words he uses to criticize Miriam are nearly identical to those Lawrence has used to characterize Paul. Paul says Miriam always looks "tight," "intense," "hurt," and "suffering," but Paul himself is said to be "tight," "screwed up" (by which Lawrence means intense), "hyper-sensitive," and "suffering."

Thus Lawrence makes us realize that whereas Paul would have Miriam believe—and, more important, have himself believe—that he and Miriam make a pair of opposites, the fact of the matter is that he and she are a great deal alike. It is in Paul's nature to "knit" the "brows" of his "soul and cogitate"; like his mother and like Miriam he possesses an intellectual spirit, a thinking soul. Indeed, if he did not, he would not be so conscious of the nature of Miriam's laugh, so aware not only of its oddness and incongruousness but also of the fact that it has been produced by her own intense awareness of an odd or incongruous thing or situation. Thus, in a sense, what Paul is speaking out against, attacking, and claiming to hate in the passage quoted above is his own self-image, which he sees all too clearly in Miriam. Throughout the novel, love and dislike and even fear turn out, on close inspection, to be forms of narcissism, self-dislike, and fear of self. Mrs. Morel feels a special pang of love for the baby Paul when she sees blue eyes that mirror her own, but later she regrets the boy's "ridiculous hypersensitiveness" because she knows the pain that her own hyper-sensitiveness has caused her. Walter Morel runs from his battered wife, but what he is really running from is himself.

Miriam senses that Paul is more like than unlike herself. She senses, especially, that his is a strong, spiritual nature, and she knows herself well enough—better than Paul knows himself, certainly—to know that she is spiritual by nature. "Miriam did not live till they came to the church," Lawrence tells us in the chapter entitled "Lad-and-Girl Love," for in "that atmosphere Miriam's soul came into a glow." Paul too "was sensitive to the feel of the place."

> Miriam turned to him. He answered. They were together. He would not go beyond the Communion-rail. She loved him for that. Her soul expanded into prayer beside him. He felt the strange fascina-tion of shadowy religious places. All his latent mysticism quivered into life. She was drawn to him. He was a prayer along with her. (167)

Here Lawrence gives us a sense of how Miriam sees Paul through indirect discourse. That is to say, the narrative remains authorial while at the same time, for a moment, presenting the world of the novel through the eyes of one of its characters. Lawrence, through his narrator, makes clear elsewhere that Paul is not, in fact, quite as "soulful" as Miriam—or as Miriam thinks he is or wishes he were. (The phrase "he was a prayer" is a hyperbole and reflects, to some extent, what Miriam wants Paul to be, not the self-contradicting bundle of opposed forces that as often as not define his character.) Still, Miriam's sense of Paul as prayer, if it is an exaggeration, is an exaggeration based on fact. In Paul, as in Miriam, the substantial, physical, instinctual, dark self most nearly epitomized by Mr. Morel is "overbalanced" by the thoughtful and soulful nature.

We have thus far focused on three of the four major characters around which Lawrence builds his novel: Walter and Gertrude Morel, unalike but bonded by marriage vows that in Lawrence's day were virtually unbreakable by members of the lower classes, and Paul Morel, bonded to his father in hate, to his mother in love. The fourth major character, Miriam Leivers, we have necessarily begun to analyze, for in Lawrence's novel of paired, opposed, and self-opposed characters, it is nearly impossible to understand one character outside the contexts provided by others.

Miriam is like Paul, but she is even more like Paul's mother, who is considerably more like Paul than Walter Morel is. Like Gertrude Morel, Miriam harbors a will to rise above the common life that she has been born into. She is proud to the point of being haughty, superior. ("Ordinary folk seemed trivial" to her [147].) And like Gertrude, she is intellectual and spiritual by nature; therefore it is through ideas and learning that she seeks to better herself: "She hated her position as swine-girl," Lawrence tells us early in chapter 7. "She wanted to be considered. She wanted to learn, thinking that if she could read . . . 'Voyage autour de ma Chambre,' the world would have a different face for her and a deepened respect. She could not be princess by wealth or standing. So she was mad to have learning whereon to pride herself" (143). Learning confirms Miriam's sense that she is "different from other folk," that she "must not be scooped up among the common fry." Thus she intends "to aspire" to the "distinction" conferred by learning (143). When she meets Paul, she finds it hard, at first, to like him, because he hurts her pride by failing to see how uncommon and intellectual she is. "The boy's poor morsel of learning exalted him almost sky-high in her esteem. Yet she tried hard to scorn him, because he would not see in her the princess but only the swine-girl" (143).

Later, however, she draws close to Paul because he can teach her poetry and French and, especially, mathematics, a subject that society defines as "male" and therefore teaches to boys, not girls. It is a mark of Miriam's aspiring nature that she wishes to learn mathematics, the very knowledge of which is proof that she can rise above her "woman's place." It is also Lawrence's way of suggesting what he has indicated through his characterization of Gertrude Morel, namely, that the roles that society prescribes to men and women often do not accord with the roles that the selves born in male and female bodies wish to play. Gertrude Morel would be happier as a theologian than John Field, but he is the one given the opportunity to prepare for the ministry.

Miriam is like Gertrude, then, because she longs to learn things reserved for men. She is like Gertrude, too, insofar as she is dominant by nature as well as proud and intellectual. She begins to feel real tenderness toward Paul when he falls ill, for she knows that, ill, "he would be weak. Then she would be stronger than he. Then she could love him. If she could be mistress of him in his weakness, take care of him, if he could depend on her, if she could, as it were, have him in her arms, how she would love him!" (143). Throughout *Sons and Lovers* we are told that Gertrude and Walter get along best when he is injured or sick. At such times, Gertrude can play the dominant role that it is in her nature to play, whereas Walter can be soft and pliable, as it is his nature to be. When Walter is not sick, Gertrude can only exercise her pride, her will, her natural toughness in the presence of other women or her own children. Because of society's definitions of proper "male" and "female" behavior, Gertrude can only successfully relate to sick or very young men. Or to young men, like Mr. Heaton, from whom she can learn.

Miriam faces exactly the same problem, which is why it is so difficult for her to love a healthy boyfriend. It would be easier for her to mold and love his children. Late in the novel Paul accuses her of not "*want*[ing] it," that is to say, the sexual union he seeks. "Don't I want your children?" she responds, as if she thinks she is answering his question. "But not me," Paul counters. "How can you say so?" she asks indignantly (291). However, the very fact that she brings up her interest in his purely hypothetical children when he questions her interest in *him* shows that he knows her fairly well. If she must think about sex, she will think about it in terms of the children it may produce, children she can dominate as well as love in a less directly physical way. Her fear of sex partly stems from her proud and independent spirit, which dislikes being dominated and knows that convention calls for a woman to be the submissive partner in sex.

It also, of course, stems partly from her overly active, never-relaxed intelligence, what Lawrence calls "consciousness" or "self-consciousness." Miriam, like Gertrude and Paul, is "tight," the opposite of a person like Walter Morel, who thoughtlessly risks his life with gaiety and is described in the opening sentence of chapter 5 as "a heedless man" (83). Because of her mental intensity, Miriam "heeds" everything. She cannot relax and enjoy physical experience. She fears for her body in a way that attests to the split in her between the mental and physical self and the extreme dominance of the former over the latter. Other children enjoy the simple pleasure of letting a chicken eat out of their hands; Miriam is described twice in five lines as "shrinking" from the experience (126). Even Paul, who is similarly tight due to hyper-consciousness, is relaxed by comparison. When the two play on a swing hung from the roof of the Leivers' family barn, Paul is shown "swinging through the air, every bit of him swinging, like a bird that swoops for joy of movement." He may not be, like his father, unafraid of literal death, but he loves to swing "negligently" and "die," speaking as the swing slows "in a detached, dreamy voice, as though he were the dying motion of the swing" (150). Miriam, on the other hand, feels "a hot wave of fear" when she takes her turn. "She gripped the rope. . . . She could never lose herself [as Paul could], nor could her brothers" (151). "All the life of Miriam's body was in her eyes,"

Lawrence tells us a few pages later. The rest of her face "scarcely ever altered from its look of brooding": thus, even her physical "look" is the look of thought. "She walked . . . heavily"; her head is "bowed" by consciousness, by "pondering. . . . There was no looseness or abandon about her. Everything was gripped stiff with intensity" (153–54).

Miriam is as spiritual as she is intellectual by nature, and is thus in yet another way likened by Lawrence with Gertrude as well as with Paul. In fact, "she was cut off from ordinary life by her religious intensity which made the world for her either a nunnery garden or a paradise, where sin and knowledge were not, or else an ugly, cruel thing" (148). Lawrence returns to the image of Miriam as a nun again and again in the novel in order to stress how spiritual—and aphysical—she is. "As Miriam sang her mouth seemed hopeless," we read in a later chapter. "She sang like a nun singing to heaven," as "spiritual"-looking as if she were a figure beside "a Botticelli Madonna" (279). By saying that her "mouth" seemed "hopeless" when she sang, Lawrence presumably means that she is tight- and thin-lipped, that there is nothing sensual, physical, about her singing. There are only melodically articulated words and meanings.

The passage is to be found in the chapter entitled "The Test on Miriam," and the "test" is one of Miriam's physical nature. Miriam passes the test in one sense while failing it in another; she proves willing to make love to Paul, but the lovemaking proves unsatisfying to both boy and girl. Thus she turns out to make love as she sings—as if she were not taking part in a physical act. She is as "hopeless" physically as she is developed spiritually and intellectually. Although she is human, she is human in the sense that a nun is. She lives in the world but is not of it. She is embodied but relatively unaware of her body as body.

Because of her unawareness of nature without and within, Lawrence seldom represents Miriam through natural beings or objects, preferring to associate her with prayers or princesses living high in fairy-tale towers and thus doubly removed from earthly realities. When he does associate her with nature, he represents her through things that are pale or white. Thus, he uses light shades or colors that deepen our sense that Miriam is profoundly like Gertrude Morel. Indeed, one scene in which Miriam particularly recalls Paul's mother is one involving white flowers like the ones with which Gertrude communed in an almost—but not quite—sexual way. Miriam is associated with white roses, not lilies, but the idea is almost exactly the same.

The scene begins as Paul sets out with Miriam to find a favorite flower bush she wants to show him: "By the time they came to the pine-trees Miriam was getting very eager and very tense. Her bush might be gone. She might not be able to find it; and she wanted it so much. Almost passionately she wanted to be with him when he stood before the flowers. They were going to have a communion together—something that thrilled her, something holy" (159). Just as in the scene in which Gertrude touches big pallid lily petals and grows dizzy in the sweet-smelling air, Lawrence here uses words that insinuate sexual meaning. (Words like "eager" and "passionately," phrases like "she wanted it" and "a communion . . . that thrilled," are obviously suggestive; even the word "bush" seems slightly suspect.) Finally, though, the very presence of such words indicates just how sublimated Miriam's sexuality is. Like Gertrude, Miriam seeks a passionate communion *like* sex but somehow at least one step beyond it, denatured of the physical, human contact that keeps it from being a transcendent spiritual communion.

For Miriam to enjoy Paul, she must enjoy him indirectly; something must be found that both she and he can appreciate simultaneously, either spiritually or aesthetically, thus allowing them to appreciate one another indirectly, without direct physical contact or communion. That something, in this scene, is the sought-for flower bush, a bush hung thick with roses that, in their whiteness and starry shape, suggest the cool pale light of heaven's high reaches. "Ah," Miriam cries almost orgasmically, "hastening forward" when she sees her bush.

> [I]ts long streamers trailed thick, right down to the grass, splashing the darkness everywhere with great spilt stars, pure white. In bosses of ivory and in large splashed stars the roses gleamed on the

darkness of foliage and stems and grass. Paul and Miriam stood close together, silent, and watched. Point after point the steady roses shone out to them, seeming to kindle something in their souls. The dusk came like smoke around, and still did not put out the roses.

Paul looked into Miriam's eyes. She was pale and expectant with wonder. . . .

She looked at her roses. They were white, some incurved and holy, others expanded in an ecstasy. . . . She lifted her hand impulsively to the flowers; she went forward and touched them in worship. (159–60)

Not unlike Gertrude Morel, whom we see touching the "dusky" gold of lily pollen but not her husband's "dusky golden softness," Miriam touches a figuratively "ecsta[tic]" white rose bush rather than a literally, physically ecstatic young man. In touching the flowers, she participates in physical communion, but only minimally, for these flowers are like "pale and expectant" Miriam herself, that is to say, they are physically "hopeless," barely embodied. "Splashing the darkness," they seem more liquid than solid, but they are more like light ("stars") than like liquid, and more like metaphysical or holy light than they are like physical light. ("The dusk came," but this liquidlike darkness could not "put out the roses.")

Characters in *Sons and Lovers*, like readers of the novel, are able to see that Miriam and Mrs. Morel are linked by certain, unmistakable likenesses. Paul, for one, sees the two women as being almost the same, virtually twins. The fact that he does, of course, partially explains why he has difficulty loving or loathing one without feeling the same way about the other. In the "Strife in Love" chapter, Lawrence provides the reader with a scene that reestablishes the connection between Gertrude and Miriam while, at the same time, reminding us that because of the likenesses, the two women are rivals competing for the affection of Paul. "The chapel was like home," Lawrence says, preparing us for a scene in which Paul is to feel, simultaneously, not only his homegrown love for his mother but also an identical love for someone who comes from outside that home. "It was a pretty place, with dark pews and slim, elegant pillars and," of course, "flowers." (Together, the pillars and flowers recall the skyward-reaching flowers that Miriam and Gertrude touch in lieu of touching a lover.) "It was wonderfully sweet and soothing to sit there for an hour and a half, next to Miriam, and near to his mother, uniting his two loves under the spell of the place of worship. Then he felt warm and happy and religious at once" (192).

One of the reasons there is a religious "feeling" about Paul's love for both Miriam and his mother is that both women are associated with Jesus Christ and the way of loving that He exemplified on the cross. (Again, Lawrence associates females with a male, quietly reminding us that, although we expect certain kinds of behavior from men and different kinds from women, the fact is that important likenesses between persons are not likely to be gender linked.) Both women love in a spirit of self-sacrifice. To the extent that they are aware of having bodies to love with, they view those bodies as things to be shared but not enjoyed. Gertrude Morel's "face" and "mouth" are described, early in the novel, as being "tight from . . . self-sacrifice" (66). Miriam, similarly, is "proud" in "sacrifice," and "in renunciation she was strong" (215). When she has sex with Paul, she is, like Christ, allowing the breaking of her body for the sole benefit of another.

> Her big brown eyes were watching him, still and resigned and loving; she lay as if she had given herself up to sacrifice: there was her body for him; but the look at the back of her eyes, like a creature awaiting immolation, arrested him, and all his blood fell back.
>
> "You are sure you want me?" he asked, as if a cold shadow had come over him.
>
> "Yes, quite sure."
>
> She was very quiet, very calm. She only realised that she was doing something for him. (289–90)

In "Lightning," a poem written in 1911 and published in the 1913 volume entitled *Love Poems and Others,* Lawrence writes about a woman similar to Miriam. "I leaned in the darkness to find her lips," says the speaker, recalling a night of unsatisfactory lovemaking:

And claim her utterly in a kiss,
When the lightning flew across her face
And I saw her for the flaring space
    Of a second, like snow that slips
From a roof, inert with death, weeping "Not this! Not this!". . .

And I heard the thunder, and felt the rain,
    And my arms fell loose, and I was dumb.
Almost I hated her, sacrificed. . . .[55]

The woman referred to in "Lightning" and Miriam may both have been inspired by Jessie Chambers, the girl who, in real life, Lawrence tried unsuccessfully to love. When we view *Sons and Lovers* as a novel, however, instead of as a key to the author's life, that fact is less important than the fact that Miriam and the woman in "Lightning" are alike, much as Miriam and Gertrude are doubled in likeness, and that, like all artists, Lawrence repeats similarities and oppositions both within a given work and throughout a career in order to create definite meaning.

The recurrence of the self-sacrificing lover in novels and poems by Lawrence suggests the following idea: in modern people, body and mind (which includes spirit and intellect) have been tragically split. Each component of the self has enough independence to dominate, overshadow, overbalance the other. In an individual overbalanced on the spiritual/intellectual side, the body is paralyzed by analysis and moral judgment. The physical/instinctual self is still there, but it is frustrated and harassed by the spiritual self, which sees it as something foreign or other. The physical nature, cut off from a dominant mental nature, comes to be seen by the latter as an embarrassment, as some-thing that needs constantly to be dominated, repressed, allowed expression only in moments that are consciously regretted as soon as they are begun. Consequently, the body can be used but not enjoyed. It can give pleasure only of the kind the martyr feels in suffering for someone else's sake or for some transcendent cause.

Paul, though not as like Miriam as Miriam is like his mother, is similarly quiescent physically, similarly overwhelmed or overbalanced mentally and spiritually. He is so mental and spiritual that he would need someone far more physical and sensual than Miriam to excite his subordinate physicality. In the "Defeat of Miriam" chapter, Paul admits that the flaw in his sexual relationship with Miriam is not all her fault. He comes to realize that two characters overbalanced on the mental/spiritual side have no future as lovers. "I can only give friendship—" he admits in a scene that offers a turnabout from the more usual situation. "[I]t's all I'm capable of—it's a flaw in my make-up. The thing *overbalances* to one side. . . . Let us have done" (221, italics mine). The careful reader earlier came to understand what Paul is only now admitting to Miriam when he said, "You see, I'm deficient in something with regard to you" (221).

Physically, Lawrence tells us in the later chapter, "The Test on Miriam," "he had no aversion for her. No, it was the opposite." Why then, if Paul's physical nature is so attracted to Miriam's, can he, like Miriam, only commune in platonic friendship? Because he has within him a self, a nature, far stronger than the physical one that has "no aversion" to her. In him "was a strong desire battling with a still stronger shyness and virginity. It seemed as if virginity were a positive force, which fought and won in both of them" (278). At this point in the story, Paul and Miriam are, literally, virgins, and yet Lawrence seems to mean more by "virginity" than sexual inexperience. The "positive" force that Lawrence calls virginity is a will to deny the body that will remain a positive force even after Paul and Miriam have made love. Virginity—the spiritual, intellectual side—goes on winning in the relationship between Miriam and Paul even after neither is, technically, virgin.

Characters in whom "virginity" is the most positive, powerful force tend to be characters associated with words, not things, in *Sons and Lovers*. We have seen the extent to which Gertrude Morel is word-oriented rather than flesh-oriented, and that Paul is similarly so, although the text he lives in is more often that of romantic poetry than of his mother's Bible. Miriam lives as much in the world of the book as do the other characters with whom she is paired in likeness. Life for her is a fiction in which she is a character. "The girl was romantic in her soul," Lawrence says at the beginning of "Lad-and-Girl Love."

> Everywhere was a Walter Scott heroine being loved by men with helmets or with plumes in their caps. She herself was something of a princess turned into a swine-girl in her own imagination. And she was afraid lest [Paul], who, nevertheless looked something like a Walter Scott hero, who could paint and speak French, and knew what algebra meant, and who went by train to Nottingham every day, might consider her simply as the swine-girl, unable to perceive the princess beneath; so she held aloof. (142)

Sometimes Miriam sees herself as a poetic, not novelistic, heroine of Sir Walter Scott's, but the causes and effects of the self-imaging are the same:

> Then she rose and went indoors. She seemed to be in some way resentful of [Paul].
> "He thinks I'm only a common girl," she thought, and she wanted to prove she was a grand person like the "Lady of the Lake." (128)

In the scene in which other children try to get Miriam to allow a hen to pluck corn from her hand, her brother alludes to her self-image as Scott's Lady of the Lake: "'Dursn't jump off a gate, dursn't tweedle, dursn't go on a slide, dursn't stop a girl hittin' her. She can do nowt but go about thinkin' herself somebody. "The Lady of the Lake." Yah!' cried Maurice" (126). Even Maurice makes the connection between Miriam's self-association with the words of a poet-novelist and her tendency not to associate herself with the world of common things and activities.

Miriam, in addition to being associated with Sir Walter Scott's Lady of the Lake, is associated by Paul with a creation of the English romantic poet William Wordsworth. Paul, who is not so purely "virgin" as Miriam, tries to interest her in more sensual, contemporary poets, such as the French writers Baudelaire and Verlaine. But

She did not like Baudelaire, on the whole—nor Verlaine.

> "Behold her singing in the field
> Yon solitary highland lass."

That nourished her heart. So did "Fair Ines." And—

> "It was a beauteous evening, calm and pure,
> And breathing holy quiet like a nun."

These were like herself. And there was he, saying in his throat bitterly:

> "*Tu te rappelleras la beauté des caresses*"
> [You remind me of the beauty of caresses]. (209)

The first indented quotation comes from Wordsworth's "The Solitary Reaper," a poem about a maiden so refreshingly pure that the poet himself needs help in deciphering her "welcome notes" or "humble lay" (ll. 10, 21). The second is from one of Wordsworth's most famous sonnets, the first eight lines of which actually read:

> It is a beauteous evening, calm and free,
> The holy time is quiet as a Nun
> Breathless with adoration; the broad sun
> Is sinking down in its tranquility;
> The gentleness of heaven broods o'er the Sea:
> Listen! the mighty being is awake,
> And doth with his eternal motion make
> A sound like thunder—everlastingly.

It is not hard to see why Miriam's "heart" would be "nourished" by a poem such as this. It is a poem that finds spiritual presence—God Himself—and not natural fact in nature, and it depicts a natural moment that is like the nun that Miriam herself resembles. Thus, it allows her a poet's glimpse of a world that accords with her own nature.

However, whereas Wordsworth says that the moment was one of freedom ("calm and free"), Miriam seems to remember him saying that the moment was one of purity ("calm and pure"). Lawrence may have intended us to see that the "overbalance" in Miriam that favors the "force" of "virginity" causes her to take a distorted view not only of nature but also of poems about the spiritual side of nature. Or, he may have simply misremembered the lines himself, making them even more "pure" and "spiritual" than they are. He may have consciously or unconsciously changed "free" to "pure" because the latter word better serves his artistic purpose, which is to represent Miriam by a fragment of literature that sees the world in the way that she does.

In either case, the passage shows us that Miriam prefers Wordsworth's poetry to the kind preferred by Paul, which sees love in terms of bodily caresses. Miriam, like the sonneteer, sees the physical world as a sign of something else of overbalancing importance, namely, the spiritual world that lies behind or beyond it. Caresses, for Miriam, are important only insofar as they are signs of a love that is spiritual. Only spiritual "facts" have reality for her; physical facts are, for the idealist (whether the idealist be Christ or Wordsworth or Plato), but shadows and dreams. Miriam "seemed as in some dreamy tale," Lawrence says in the chapter on "Lad-and-Girl Love," "her spirit dreaming in a land far away and magical" (145). That faraway, magical land, however, is more real to Miriam than life on the farm, which is the "dreamy tale." "[H]er discoloured, old blue frock and her broken boots seemed only like the romantic rags of King Cophetua's beggar-maid" (145). The cold hard facts of life, in other words, are to Miriam false, like disguises in a fairy tale. The truth about her identity is the faraway land that the "positive" force of "virginity"—her intensely intellectual/spiritual nature—takes her to.

Thus Lawrence associates both Miriam and Paul with words. Indeed, he grounds their very relationship in languages: of English and French literature and of mathematical signs. At the same time, he differentiates slightly between the kinds of language preferred by each character. Thus, he simultaneously compares and contrasts these two young people whose failed romance is plotted by the central chapters of his novel. Paul, like Miriam, is more "mental"—more prone to intellectual and spiritual matters and to the world of the word—than to living the physical life in a world of things. But he is less overbalanced by the mental side than Miriam, which is to say he is a more evenly divided self. Miriam is drawn to two poems by Wordsworth that are, respectively, about a girl whose poetic identity is a song and about a world whose purpose is to serve as a temple of God. ("Thou liest in Abraham's bosom all the year," Wordsworth says to his sister in the eleventh line of "It Is a Beauteous Evening," and he concludes the sonnet by telling her that she "worshipp'st at the Temple's inner shrine" while merely living in nature.) Paul may be more prone to making up poems about caresses than to actually caressing a lover, but he is more inclined toward the poetry of caresses—and to fairly sensual writers such as Baudelaire and Verlaine—than he is to the calmer, purer poetry of the type that Miriam likes. The very fact that he is prone to write words about touch reveals the dichotomy that is in Paul.

That dichotomy is, to a great extent, responsible for the tragic tension that finally destroys the relationship between these two people, who are far more alike than opposite one another. We have seen the divided self before in Walter and Gertrude Morel: Walter is mainly physical and therefore amoral but at times eaten away at by the "rust" of moral consciousness; Gertrude is mainly moral and intellectual, but a relatively small "part of her" is drawn to her sensual, amoral husband in spite of his stupidity and brutality. Paul, however, is a more severely divided self than either of his parents. He is, after all, a product of two people who, though somewhat divided within, are quite decisively "overbalanced" in favor of opposite forces, namely, the physical/sensual force that controls Walter and the intellectual/spiritual force of "virginity" that guides Gertrude.

Paul is, as well, a more severely divided self than Miriam, which is not to say that she does not have two (or more) selves to contend with. Overbalanced though she may be in favor of coldness, rigidity, pride, intellect, and puritanical spiritualism, she is not entirely deficient in unconscious, instinctive, amoral, sensual forces—for no one, in Lawrence's world, is. Indeed, words like *overbalanced* and *deficient* themselves imply the presence of those very things that Miriam is short of but, by definition, not without. "It was spring, which she loved and dreaded," Lawrence says in one suggestive passage (216). Miriam's love for Paul begins because of a "common feeling for something in Nature," and we cannot, at times, be entirely sure that that "something" is spiritual (148). When once she watches his hands working on a punctured bicycle tire, she experiences pleasure sensually, unselfconsciously. She suddenly "realise[s]" "the male he [is]" and wants "to run her hands down his sides" (189). Lawrence suggests the contradiction in Miriam by connecting her physical looks with those of Walter Morel, not Paul and Gertrude. Paul and his mother are pale and delicate looking with cool blue eyes; Miriam, by contrast, has a face that Lawrence describes as being "rosy dark" at one point. Thus, Lawrence associates her with red and black, the colors of fire and coal, passion and the unconscious life with which Paul's father is associated (124). Also, Miriam's face is distinguished not by blue but rather by "dark eyes," and it is framed by "black curls, very fine and free" (124). (The curls, when used in association with the word *free*, once again remind us not of Paul or his mother but, rather, of Walter, whose "wavy black hair" accords well with the temper of a man who *"can't* understand rules and regulation" [87].) Even the "flush[es]" that regularly warm and redden Miriam's face, though they may be caused by an embarrassment that attests to moral consciousness, at the same time suggest physical energies that are overbalanced by the mental, moral forces.

Still, Miriam does, mainly, want soul union with Paul, because "virginity" is a far more powerful, positive force in her than is that tendency to unselfconscious physical abandon suggested by those occasional scenes in which "warmth" is said to be "roused" in her. Paul is more like than unlike Miriam, but because he is the product of an extremely anarchic, sensual nature as well as a strongly puritanical one, he is more often swayed by his usually dominated physical/instinctual side. Indeed, there are times in Paul's life when the "father" in him is in ascendancy, and during those moments he seems more like Walter Morel, whom he usually is "peculiarly *against*," than like his mother (58). Even in the early chapter devoted to "The Young Life of Paul," there is a scene that associates Paul with the man he is usually opposed to: Walter Morel, who "loved a fire dearly." Paul "loved the evenings, after eight o'clock, when the light was put out, and he could watch the fire-flames spring over the darkness of the walls and ceiling; could watch huge shadows waving and tossing, till the room seemed full of men who battled silently" (66). Evening, the extinguishing of light, fire-flames, darkness, waving and tossing, silence, and battle—all these words and phrases and ideas are associated with Walter, the wavy-haired man of violence and few words who eats dinner late in a room lit only by the light of the fire.

Paul, at times, even shares his father's vitality. His mother "had never expected him to live," and yet, the novel tells us, "he had a great vitality in his young body. Perhaps it would have been a little relief to her if he had died" (66). (The last sentence is a curious one. Why would Gertrude Morel—or part of her, anyway—want her son to die? It may be because Paul, in his vitality, reminds her of her husband, and her husband is someone whose death would, "perhaps" or partly, come as a relief to her.) Paul's nonintellectual vitality is apparent when he swings "like a bird that swoops with joy of movement" (150). At other points, Paul's vital energies break out of him in acts of violence. He eerily resembles his father while, of all things, teaching Miriam algebra. Her slowness in learning causes "his blood" to "beg[i]n to boil with her. It was strange that no one else made him in such fury. He flared against her. Once he threw the pencil in her face" (157). An uncharacteristic moment? Yes, Lawrence would say, and no: yes because Paul is predominantly, like his mother, a paragon of self-conscious self-control. He is not predominantly, as his father is, either physical by nature or heedless of consequences. And yet his father is present in him as part of his make-up. Just as someone like his mother can contain selves or aspects of self that society would define as "male" and "female," so can someone like Paul suddenly stop being his mother, stop being ruled by the force of "virginity," and start being ruled by another force over which his conscious, mental self seems to have little control.

This other force, associated with his father and not (for the most part) with his mother, is, of course, more prone to sensuality than to violence. It is Paul's "fatherly" nature that is strongly attracted to Clara Dawes, Miriam Leivers's opposite or foil in *Sons and Lovers*. Miriam is baffled by Paul's "passion" for Clara, who is as overbalanced by the physical/instinctive nature as Miriam is by the intellectual/spiritual side. When asked what it is he likes about this married woman, Paul answers Miriam by saying, "I don't know—her skin and the texture of her—and her—I don't know—there's a sort of fierceness somewhere in her. I appreciate her as an artist, that's all" (187). It is significant that Paul stammers out his response to Miriam's request that he analyze his feelings for Clara. Feelings that arise in the sensual/instinctive nature are foreign to mental consciousness and cannot be analyzed. Even if they could be, they would be difficult to put into words, which neither arise from nor accurately describe those zones of existence Lawrence associates with darkness and with blood. Clara, like Walter Morel, is mainly an inhabitant of the world of things and of the body. She is appreciated by the father in Paul and not well described by words, which Paul's father is hardly a master of. She would be better described by a Baudelaire or a Verlaine than a Wordsworth, but she is even better represented by palpable daubs of paint on a physical canvas. It is the painter—not the poet—in Paul that appreciates her.

Thus, even Paul's artistic nature is supported by forces that are more like those dominant in his father than in his mother. Earlier we examined the scene in which Walter Morel's unselfconscious, free nature caused him to look for a moment like the artist—not the kind of cerebral artist who writes a novel like James Joyce's *Ulysses* or T. S. Eliot's *The Waste Land* but, rather, like the kind of potter or sculptor who is creative in molding wet clay or hot metal. When repairing boots or mending kettles or his "pit-bottle," he "hammered the soft, red-glowing stuff on his iron goose" and made whatever "shape he wanted" (63). When Paul repairs his bicycle tire, he recalls his father at work in the scullery:

> When he went into the barn for his bicycle he found the front wheel punctured.

"Fetch me a drop of water in a bowl," he said to her. "I shall be late, and then I s'll catch it."

He lighted the hurricane lamp, took off his coat, turned up the bicycle, and set speedily to work. Miriam came with the bowl of water and stood close to him, watching. She loved to see his hands doing things. He was slim and vigorous, with a kind of easiness even in his most hasty movements. And busy at his work he seemed to forget her. (189)

The image of a lamp burning in the darkness recalls Walter Morel, as does the image of Paul pouring himself into his work to the point of becoming heedless of everything else. (The scene reminds us not only of the one in which the elder Morel works in the scullery but also the one in which he strikes away at a coal vein as if unaware of the fact that the working day has ended and everyone else has gone home.) Even Paul's language ("I s'll catch it") suddenly sounds like his father's. When Paul's physical/instinctual side dominates, in other words, he becomes less a creature of the literary "word." When the intellectual/ spiritual side dominates, "correct" words become more useful. Paul sometimes speaks in dialect, but more often with the "proper" English spoken by his mother. To some degree, he adjusts his language to ac- cord with that of the people he is talking to, and yet there are many scenes in which he speaks properly to a character who speaks dialect and many other scenes—such as this one—in which he speaks crudely to a refined character. That is because Paul's makeup contains several natures. Lawrence sometimes lets us know that Walter Morel's nature is being expressed in Paul by having Paul sound, suddenly, more like his father's child than his mother's.

Thus, whereas Lawrence usually uses novelistic strategies to as- sociate Paul with his mother while contrasting him with his father, sometimes he uses color (black), imagery (fire), Paul's manner of speaking ("I s'll"), or an action scene (such as the one in which Paul throws a pencil at Miriam or works on a bicycle tire as if unconscious of everything else) to make a connection entirely contrary to the usual ones. Having fixed the tire at Miriam's, Paul rides home in the way his father would ride, feeling what his father would feel: "His bicycle seemed to fall beneath him, and he loved it. Recklessness is almost a man's revenge on his woman. He feels he is not valued, so he will risk destroying himself to deprive her altogether" (190). The moment is a rare one in the novel, for it is one that, by helping us understand Paul, helps us to understand his father. (We suddenly realize that Walter, who "feels he is not valued," drinks and injures himself in the mine in order to "deprive" his wife "altogether.") Usually insights gained into Paul and his mother run parallel. Here Lawrence works at cross-purpose, and he does so to show that Paul, like all human beings, has a fairly definable nature and yet, at the same time, another nature that is entirely contrary to the dominant one.

Because he does, Paul can even look unlike himself. That is to say, he can look like his father. The most powerful example of Lawrence's effort to make Paul look, occasionally, unlike his usual self is to be found, appropriately, in the "Strife in Love" chapter. (The location is appropriate since, obviously, vacillations of selfhood or identity create great strains in relationships, which are usually built upon each partner's attraction to certain characteristics of the other. When those characteristics give way to opposite ones, the relationship must change or die.) The catalyst of the scene is Beatrice, a forward, sexy, almost animalistic "vixen," who combs Paul's hair in Miriam's presence. Beatrice, not unlike Clara Dawes, has a physical, sensual nature that seems to bring out the "father" in Paul and cause the mother to retreat invisibly within:

> "Light, old boy?" said Beatrice, tilting her cigarette at him.
>
> He bent forward to her to light his cigarette at hers. She was winking at him as he did so. Miriam saw his eyes trembling with mischief, and his full, almost sensual, mouth quivering. *He was not himself, and she could not bear it. As he was now, she had no connection with him; she might as well not have existed.* She saw the cigarette dancing on his full red lips. She hated his thick hair for being tumbled loose on his forehead. (204–5, italics mine).

The miner with the "red, moist mouth" and "wavy black hair" is suddenly standing before Miriam Leivers. Gertrude Morel ended up married to that man, in spite of the fact that she had precious little "connection with him." Miriam is a more modern, intellectual woman and will not make the same mistake.

Thus, one side of Paul may be enhanced or encouraged by the presence of another person who closely resembles that side. Miriam, of course, brings out the opposite side of Paul from the side encouraged by Beatrice or Clara Dawes. That does not mean, though, that the physical side of his nature is totally dormant in Miriam's presence, for he cannot help but be aware that this young woman, who demands intellectual, soulful communion, also has "the most beautiful body he had ever imagined" (289). Because she has such a body, Miriam—who is as predominantly intellectual and spiritual as she looks physical—intensifies Paul's sense of self-conflict:

> Sometimes, as they were walking together, she slipped her arm timidly into his. But he always resented it, and she knew it. It caused a violent conflict in him. With Miriam he was always on the high plane of abstraction, when his natural fire of love was transmitted into the fine steam of thought. . . .
> Then, if she put her arm in his, it caused him almost torture. His consciousness seemed to split. (173)

As the passage above demonstrates, the split consciousness suffered to a greater or lesser degree by all the characters in *Sons and Lovers* causes pain, even "torture," to the individual whose consciousness is split. The individual in pain, in turn, projects his or her suffering into relationships, which are made more difficult than they might otherwise have been. The split in Walter Morel pits the man's "inner consciousness" against his gay, amoral spirit, and the former eats into the latter "like rust" (41). Drunkenness results from this split consciousness, as do related acts of physical violence that give the moral nature more to hate about its amoral counterpart. An even better example of the internal and external pain caused by self-conflict or split consciousness is provided in a scene involving Mr. and Mrs. Morel, each of whom contains a self that likes a side of its mate, each of whom contains a self that does not: "Dismissed, he wanted to kiss her, but he dared not. She half wanted him to kiss her, but could not bring herself to give any sign. She only breathed freely when he was gone out of the room again, leaving behind him a faint smell of pit-dirt" (33). Part of Gertrude is drawn to her husband, while another part is repelled, just as part of Paul is attracted while another part is repelled by Miriam's wish for a lover who is a "fine steam of thought" (173).

In the two instances cited above, feelings of attraction and repulsion are experienced more or less simultaneously and thus counterbalance one another. Sometimes, however, opposed feelings succeed one another in waves. Thus, rather than "half want[ing]" to kiss and half wanting not to, rather than loathing physically while loving spiritually, characters vacillate back and forth at different times between one sort of love for one side of a partner and a different sort of love for another, very different side. "How he hated her!" Lawrence says of Paul in the "Strife in Love" chapter. "And then, what a rush of tenderness and humility!" (193).

In some ways, this vacillation of selves does more harm to relationships than the more static condition of counterbalanced forces, for just when one partner tries to respond to the hatred in another by changing his or her own role, the person doing the hating may begin to love what was only a moment ago hated and therefore to hate the partner for having made a radical adjustment. To follow up one form of hatred immediately with another, inconsistent form is, of course, cruel (*cruel* is a word that appears often in *Sons and Lovers*), and cruelty in turn inflicts pain that provokes another adjustment or response—a response that may, itself, be cruelly intended. Thus this cycle of suffering and cruelty, which begins within as a war between selves, is reflected outward in such a way as to become self-perpetuating.

It is important to reiterate the fact that outward conflicts between men and women, women and women, and men and men begin within, where the modern self is fundamentally fragmented. Many novelists before Lawrence, after all, depicted cycles of cruelty and retribution; Lawrence's achievement lies in suggesting that there is a tragic tension inside the self—between primordial instinct and modern Western reason, between sensuality and a counterforce called "virginity," even between "male" and "female" habits and yearnings—that produces tragic conflicts without. These conflicts may erupt between divided selves within marriages, but they are also waged on battlefields. (The incipience of a world war, though barely alluded to in *Sons and Lovers*, is one of the things happening just off the edge of the landscape depicted in the novel. Lawrence makes the allusions because the theater of war is directly connected to the domestic drama of divided selves that forms his more immediate subject.)

To summarize the cause of the dramatic conflict between Paul and Miriam, then, we could say that one side of Paul, split off from his other side, assumes dominance and sees its foreign counterpart mirrored outwardly in Miriam, toward whom it therefore acts hatefully. (It is clearly suggested again and again by Lawrence that Paul's dislike of Miriam is inseparable from his own negative self-image. "Was *he* deficient in something?" Paul wonders, just after complaining about Miriam's all-too-soulful love of him [221].) It is easier to dislike a feared deficiency in one's self by calling it someone else's deficiency, and that is exactly what Paul does. He "hated her bitterly," Lawrence tells us on the next page (222), as if he has not just wondered if the fault lies within. Hatred of "Miriam's" deficiency, however, inevitably breeds more self-contempt, for however Paul may want to ignore the fact that he, too, is "under"-balanced on the sensual side, his sensual side or "blood consciousness" will not let him forget. Growing self-contempt leads to growing cruelty toward Miriam. Or rather it does until the more soulful, spiritual side of Paul suddenly takes over and despises its sensual, amoral, and often cruel counterpart.

The sudden ascendancy of the forces of intellect, morality, spirituality, or what Paul refers to as "virginity," however, does not guarantee cessation of pain for Miriam. After all, the rational, moral, mental side of Paul's character is perfectly capable of doing the opposite of what its counterpart has earlier done. That is to say, it may see its foreign counterpart mirrored outwardly in Miriam and therefore act hatefully toward her. Miriam, after all, has a sensual look, a flush to her skin, a beautiful warm coloring, and even a side of her that, were it not for its dominant counterpart, would cause Miriam to run her hands over Paul's body. The mother in Paul, who is aware of the dark father in him and who lives in conflict with that father within, is also aware of and hostile to the presence of Miriam's dark, red, sensual self. And it is just as capable of treating Miriam cruelly for looking sensual as the sensual, amoral, father within is capable of treating her cruelly for seeming so soulful. Thus, the cyclic alterations between self-loathing and cruelty, between cruelty and pain and more cruelty, are really only parts of a larger, cyclical alteration between cruelties inflicted and pains suffered by alternate selves for opposite reasons. Lawrence summarizes this highly complex process of alterations tersely in a passage that begins as Miriam defines God as mentality or consciousness. Paul's sensual side—the father in him—cannot believe that God is hyperconscious and self-conscious, like the mother in him. Surely God is "gay" and "heedless":

> "I don't believe God knows such a lot about Himself," he cried. "God doesn't *know* things, He *is* things. And I'm sure He's not soulful."
>
> And then it seemed to her that Paul was arguing God on to his own side, because he wanted his own way and his own pleasure.

Miriam is only half right. It is only a side of Paul that is arguing God to its own side. There is another side of Paul that is highly conscious, moral. That side is capable of shame and repentance and prone to have perfectly conventional feelings. It will have its day, eventually, but only for awhile. The passage continues: "There was a long battle between him and her. He was utterly unfaithful to her even in her own presence; then he was ashamed, then repentant; then he hated her, and went off again. *Those were the ever-recurring conditions*" (251, italics mine). Lawrence could hardly make clearer that the "long battle" between Paul and Miriam is the outward reflection of a battle within Paul, a battle between a shameless sensual self and a sensitive moral one that continually take turns coming to the forefront and then going off again, leaving control of Paul to the other. The battle with Miriam may come to an end, for the Miriam without can be "defeated" and abandoned. The Miriam (or Gertrude) within, however, cannot be so easily jettisoned. And the inner battle between Miriam and Paul, between the "father" and "mother" in him, will go on until Paul dies. For in death the physical, wholly embodied father will cease and return to the earth, its element.

6

THE WASTE LAND
ACCORDING TO
D. H. LAWRENCE
Social Forms of
Conflict and Self-Conflict

In "The Burial of the Dead," the opening movement of T. S. Eliot's modernist classic *The Waste Land* (1922), a speaker speaking in English is interrupted by a disembodied voice speaking in German:

> Summer surprised us, coming over the Starnbergersee
> With a shower of rain; we stopped in the colonnade,
> And went on in sunlight, into the Hofgarten,
> And drank coffee, and talked for an hour.
> Bin gar keine Russin, stamm' aus Litauen, echt deutsch.
> And when we were children, staying at the archduke's,
> My cousin's, he took me out on a sled,
> And I was frightened. (ll. 8–15)

The speaker of the line in German is saying that he is not a Russian, for he comes from Lithuania and is, therefore, a true German. The line, foreign to those in English that surround it, quietly suggests the foreignness, the near-identitylessness, of all modern men and women. The Great War has dislocated peoples by redefining boundaries, confusing identities in the process, fragmenting peoples who truly share a culture and bringing others together who, sometimes literally, cannot communicate. The poetic passage is fragmented, confused, by the line in German; the speaker of the line believes himself to be the victim of confused notions about the identity of his homeland, which lies fragmented by national boundaries; as for the "Marie" who tells of sledding at the archduke's, she turns out to be disoriented as well. "I read much of the night, and go south in the winter," she concludes her remarks by saying (l. 18). Even the reader feels confused by, cut off from, the text. Is Marie the same person who spoke earlier of stopping in the colonnade for coffee and talk? There is no way of telling.

A world so fragmented, confused, and even fearful is a sterile, arid world of waste, and it is just such a desert that Eliot criticizes in *The Waste Land:*

> What are the roots that clutch, what branches grow
> Out of this stony rubbish? Son of man,
> You cannot say, or guess, for you know only
> A heap of broken images, where the sun beats,
> And the dead tree gives no shelter, the cricket no relief,
> And the dry stone no sound of water. (ll. 19–24)

"I will show you fear in a handful of dust," this voice says six lines later, just before being cut off by four lines of singing in German.

Sons and Lovers, written before England declared war on Germany, seems far removed in style, spirit, and setting from the *The Waste Land,* a poem composed of a medley of the sometimes cacophonous voices of dislocated, Continental moderns. Shortly after publishing the novel, however, Lawrence came to know firsthand many of the problems of isolation, alienation, dislocation, and even fear written about by Eliot. In 1914, Lawrence married Frieda von Richthofen, a cousin of Manfred von Richthofen, the World War One flying ace who became better known as the "Red Baron." Following the marriage—and the war's outbreak—Lawrence suffered many of the difficulties alluded to by Eliot in poems such as *The Waste Land:* painful difficulties and divisions caused by war, dislocation, and the communication barriers that result from estrangement. The

Lawrences' marriage was violently shaken, their tranquillity disturbed owing to the fact that they were not trusted, were seen by the British people as aliens—Frieda because she was "one of them" and Lawrence because he had married one. According to local suspicion, the German baroness and her dangerous, "pornographer" husband were communicating with and possibly even providing food and fuel for German submarines cruising off Zenner, the Cornish seaside town in which the couple lived during the war. On 11 October 1917, the Lawrences' cottage was ransacked by police looking for evidence that the two were spies; on 12 October, an army officer ordered the Lawrences out of Cornwall, further stipulating that they could not make their home near any area deemed sensitive by the government and that they had to report to the police whenever they were planning a move.

To suggest that Lawrence's life bears better witness than *Sons and Lovers* to the kinds of social problems that T. S. Eliot alludes to— fragmentation, alienation, cultural aridity, and spiritual waste—is not to say that Lawrence has nothing critical to say, in 1912–13, about the society that he watched develop during the later years of the nineteenth century and the early years of the twentieth. Indeed, from the first page of the novel, Lawrence contrasts the dusty, black and grey, meaningless life of mining families living in the Bottoms with the life of a lost idyllic world, one in which there were injustices but also romantic heroes and heroines to counterbalance them. Not unlike Marie, who contrasts the seasons of her present with a lost childhood of romance and adventure, Lawrence critiques the tawdry, meaningless lives of the mining families by reminding us that their vapid lives are led on the edge of Sherwood Forest, where merry men and maids once roamed free.

Since *Sons and Lovers* is more than somewhat autobiographical, it is only natural that Lawrence would take as his setting the Nottinghamshire of his youth. The naturalness of the choice of setting, however, should not obscure the fact that it is the novelist in Lawrence who chooses to call attention to the fact that this is the same area of England once roamed by Robin Hood. The artist calls attention to that fact, furthermore, in order to underline a point ironically. The point is that Merry Old England has disappeared, given way to an inferior, dry, mechanized new England. In the following passage, quoted earlier, Lawrence deliberately holds his allusion to the legendary history of the area like a trump card, playing it in the last two words of the paragraph: "Then, some sixty years ago, a sudden change took place. The gin-pits were elbowed aside by the large mines of the financiers. The coal and iron field of Nottinghamshire and Derbyshire was discovered. Carston, Waite and Co. appeared. Amid tremendous excitement, Lord Palmerston formally opened the company's first mine at Spinney Park, on the edge of Sherwood Forest" (1). The change, however exciting at first, is not entirely for the better. With the coming of pits and trains, other impractical things of the spirit and imagination—such as legends and vows of faith—come to seem relics of a forever lost past: "Carston, Waite & Co. found they had struck on a good thing, so, down the valleys of the brooks from Selby and Nuttall, new mines were sunk, until soon there were six pits working. From Nuttall, high up on the sandstone among the woods, the railway ran, past the ruined priory of the Carthusians and past Robin Hood's Well . . . : six mines like black studs on the countryside, linked by a loop of fine chain, the railway" (1–2). Even nature seems somehow subordinate to the world that has been dug out below it. Agricultural fields, once crucial to the ongoing life of the area, now are excavated here, used as railway beds there. "Minton," one of the six "studs on the countryside," is "a large mine among corn-fields; from Minton across the farmlands of the valleyside to Bunker's Hill" the railway runs to Beggarlee and Selby, two of the other coal-yielding wounds in the landscape.

Where fields are not being excavated or cut across by railroad tracks, they are being built upon willy-nilly to accommodate the inflow of miners and their families. Lawrence thought "the Squares, great quadrangles of dwellings on the hillside of Bestwood" built by the mining companies for their laborers, an offense to the landscape (2). As we also know, he offers an even sharper critique of the inside of the homes than he does of the outside. Indeed, from the outside, the individual houses seem "decent," having as they do "little front gardens, . . . neat front windows, little porches, little privet hedges, and dormer windows for the attics."

> But that was outside; that was the view on to the uninhabited parlours of all the colliers' wives. The dwelling-room, the kitchen, was at the back of the house, facing inward between the blocks, looking at a scrubby back garden, and then at the ash-pits. And between the rows, between the long lines of ash-pits, went the alley, where the children played and the women gossiped and the men smoked. (2)

"So," Lawrence pointedly reiterates, "the actual conditions of living in the Bottoms, that was so well built and that looked so nice, were quite unsavoury because people must live in the kitchen, and the kitchens opened on to that nasty alley of ash-pits" (2).

I have argued, as many critics have, that Lawrence was neither a socialist nor a prototypical fascist. Nevertheless, we can hardly avoid the conclusion that the novelist's heavily implied criticism of the housing built by Carston, Waite and Co. implies a critique of capitalism itself, for it suggests that the profit motive has replaced those more generous motives of the Carthusians, of Robin Hood. Any appearance of concern for the conditions in which people live, the passage quoted above implies, is just that—only an appearance. As long as the life led by the miners and their wives looks "decent" and "neat" on the outside, the "unsavoury" inside life—the life that goes on in the ash-pits behind—matters little. Thus, although the social conditions of life in the Bottoms look fair enough from the outside, they have been constructed to appear that way. But the gardens and parlors in front are "uninhabited"; as such, they are all show, symbols of the mining company's bad faith. Life is lived at the back of the homes. That is where men smoke when they are home, when they are not at the pub relieving the tedium of their lives with alcohol. Wives, the poorest of the poor, live lives confined to the kitchen, with their children, not far from the trash, the garbage, the charred waste that cannot be seen from the house fronts. Their words are confined to gossip.

The Waste Land According to D. H. Lawrence

Lawrence's vision of life in the ash pits is not all that different from Eliot's vision of modern society as a wasteland. The evening vision of men smoking and women gossiping in between the backs of the brick houses is not unlike Eliot's vision, in an early poem entitled "Preludes" (1917), of "the burnt-out ends of smoky days" (l. 4). Eliot pictures men with "short square fingers stuffing pipes" and "women / Gathering fuel in vacant lots" instead of gossiping, but the idea of waste and meaninglessness conveyed by Eliot is quite close to that implied by Lawrence (l. 43, ll. 53–54). Furthermore, in other poems published in the same volume as "Preludes," Eliot uses gossip much as Lawrence does to convey the absence from modern life of significance, purpose, or romance. Lawrence's women, unlike the women alluded to in Eliot's poem "The Love Song of J. Alfred Prufrock," may not "come and go / Talking of Michelangelo," but their talk is equally trivial.

Just as characters have two sides, then, a visible side and a more passive, invisible one that at points erupts to the surface, so social life has a front and back, an inside and outside, a street running along the house fronts and another connecting the houses along the back. Does the manufactured duplicity of the capitalist social structure, the engineered division between the way things seem and are, have anything to do with the divisions that we have been concentrating on in this study? Are the conflicts between soul and intellect, female and male, instinct and "virginity" that exist within the novel's characters manufactured by industrial organizations, capitalist institutions and conventions? The best answer to the question seems to be yes—and no. To some extent, Lawrence seems to think that the human self is, naturally, a complex coexistence of separate selves. At the same time, he seems to believe that institutions create even more selves, selves that are false and not natural. They also produce conflicts without and within, that is to say, they worsen conflicts between natural selves, selves that would otherwise coexist more easily.

The development of mining and manufacturing in a region such as Nottinghamshire was not, of course, all bad, as Lawrence would have known perfectly well. Indeed, if the men living in the Bottoms had not had their dangerous, underground work to do, then many of them would have had no work at all (and neither would the men and women who made artificial limbs and stockings for them). The development of railways in England and America had severely hurt English agriculture, for trains had made it possible for farmers in Illinois and Kansas to ship their wheat overseas. American agricultural produce could be sold at much lower rates than British foodstuffs, which were produced on tiny farms such as the one that Miriam Leivers grew up on. Still, Lawrence suggests, the kinds of work that miners and assembly line workers do, and the ways in which they are expected to perform their tasks, contribute to the mechanization of the individual. The dehumanization of work, in turn, contributes to the kind of self-division that we have called the split between mental and physical selves. For what has the mind to do with a body whose functions are prescribed by rules, dictated by clocks and whistles and bells? Why should not the soul and imagination save themselves by pulling away from such a mechanized instrument?

We have already seen the ways in which miners' lives are mechanized. Walter Morel is the only miner we meet whose work is a passion, something his own to do. He is the only one who hates to be constrained by rules and regulations, who stops doing a job because he is finished and not because it is two o'clock. Coal miners, however, are not the only ones whose bodies have been turned into robotic machines, men whose minds are therefore free to dissociate and wander away from bodies doing impersonal work. Even Paul, for all the creativity he inherits from his father, for all the intense consciousness he inherits from his mother, is at times turned into little more than an automaton by the job he does during the day. Even before he finds his job at Jordan's Surgical Appliances—during the weeks in which he searches for a job—Paul "looked wistfully out of the window. Already he was a prisoner of industrialism. Large sunflowers stared over the old red wall of the garden opposite, looking in their jolly way down on the women who were hurrying with something for dinner. The valley was full of corn, brightening in the sun. . . . He was being taken into bondage. His freedom in the beloved home valley was going now" (89). Once again, in *Sons and Lovers,* a flower serves as the outward symbol of inner self or soul. The sunflower represents Paul's past gaiety and heedlessness, the relative freedom and naturalness of the self he knew before being sentenced to the prison of industrialism. (It is, significantly, neither a passionate red nor a pure white flower but, rather, something in between.) That gaiety, or we could call it freedom or heedlessness, has a place in nature, even in one of the little gardens along the uninhabited fronts of a miner's house. It has no place, however, in the workplace. It will have to separate itself from Paul's day-to-day life.

Paul is, a few pages later, employed at Jordan's, and we discover why the sunflowerlike "jollity" of a person has to be divorced from the workday life. Paul has refused to follow his father into the miner's life, and yet, ironically, life above ground proves no more rewarding. Like a miner, Paul is reduced and numbed by his job, which is the opposite of a creative one. He merely reproduces the (trivial) work of others. " 'Come, my lad,' " Mr. Pappleworth urges "imploringly to Paul, 'there's Polly crying out for them orders.' " The very name of the girl crying out for paper forms suggests the uncreative, unoriginal, subhuman—"parroting"—nature of work at Jordan's. "Can't you buck up a bit?" Pappleworth continues:

> "Here, come out!"
> He took the book, to Paul's immense chagrin, and began the copying himself. He worked quickly and well. This done, he seized some strips of long yellow paper, about three inches wide, and made out the day's orders for the work-girls. (104)

By "orders" Lawrence refers, primarily, to orders that need to be filled. But the word may be taken in another sense, too, for the manufacturing workplace is one in which, because people merely obey orders, the creative or imaginative or spiritual capacity is useless. Even Paul, the women's boss, and Mr. Pappleworth, Paul's boss, are only involved in copying. The work they do would today be done by a photocopying machine. They merely "poll parrot" letters passed on to them, turning them then into a list of orders to be passed on to the women.

It is, of course, a biographical fact that the young D. H. Lawrence worked at J. H. Haywood's, Manufacturer of Surgical Appliances, a place much like Jordan's Surgical Appliances. Still, we cannot fail to see the symbolic importance of the products—prostheses or "wooden legs"—and accessories made and shipped by Jordan's. The "flesh pink 'leg' " that Paul is shown just before he is introduced to the women who work in "the finishing room" suggests all too clearly the idea that modern work can dehumanize men and women, rob them of their jollity, and turn them into mechanized likenesses of real, complete human beings. Workers who are made into incomplete, partial selves are deformed by their employers. The hunchbacked body of the girl named Fanny, like the wooden legs sold by Jordan's, implies the deformation of human nature created by work that requires a "finish" of a certain, prescribed type, work that causes the creative spirit of the worker either to wither and die or to seek escape from the mindlessly physical labor that the body is doing. The scene in which Paul meets the six young women who work in the finishing room tersely suggests the need of mind or spirit to escape from the body doing rote, manufacturing labor. Having walked through a "door whence" a "girl had emerged, . . . Paul found himself at the top of a little wooden flight of steps, and below him saw a room with windows round two sides, and at the farther end half a dozen girls sitting bending over the benches in the light from the window, sewing. They were singing together 'Two Little Girls in Blue.' Hearing the door opened, they all turned round, to see Mr. Pappleworth and Paul looking down on them. . . . They stopped singing" (106–7). With the arrival of one who gives "orders," the fanciful song of escape is brought to a halt. The six women turn round at once, almost as if they were puppets assembled from parts and elastics manufactured at the plant that employs them. That is, moreover, exactly what Mr. Pappleworth wants them to be. To Lawrence's mind a man like Pappleworth is asking his workers to be, like himself, less than fully human, but as the following passage clearly and ironically shows, Mr. Pappleworth is a company man and holds to quite a different philosophy: " 'Can't you make a bit less row?' said Mr. Pappleworth. 'Folk'll think we keep cats.' " (107). Men whose job it is to think such perverse thoughts are dehumanized along with the

women they oppress, and although Paul never becomes a Mr. Pappleworth (he has too much of his father in him to like "orders," whether
they are given or obeyed), he is forced by the work situation into de-
nying his true identity and adopting a false one.

Thus, in a sense, the manufacturing workplace, which dictates
that young men will manage and give orders and do paperwork and
tell young women what to do, causes self-division by making men and
women assume selves, adopt roles or identities, that may not be natural or right for them. There is no real or rational or natural reason
why Clara Dawes, who works for a while at Jordan's, should obey
orders given by Paul. She is older, married, intelligent, and his lover.
Social and company conventions, however, dictate just such a relationship, and whereas Clara wants to be the same person at work that
she is away, Paul insists on the self-division that will allow him to be
a worker's boss during the daylight hours and a woman's lover by
night. The following passage painfully describes Clara as she works at
knitting elastic stockings and bandages on a spiral machine in "the
Spiral room" and thinks how much she would like Paul to be himself
at work and to treat her like herself:

> Every second she expected him to come through the door, and when
> he came it was a shock to her. But he was often short and offhand
> with her. He gave her his directions in an official manner, keeping
> her at bay. With what wits she had left she listened to him. She
> dared not misunderstand or fail to remember, but it was a cruelty
> to her. She wanted to touch his chest. She knew exactly how his
> breast was shapen under the waistcoat, and she wanted to touch it.
> It maddened her to hear his mechanical voice giving orders about
> the work. She wanted to break through the sham of it, smash the
> trivial coating of business which covered him with hardness, get at
> the man again; but she was afraid, and before she could feel one
> touch of his warmth he was gone, and she ached again. (351)

A "mechanical" man at work, Paul treats Clara like an animal ("keeping her at bay"). That does not mean, however, that he can allow her
to express her physical self, for he can no more do so than he can
permit himself to be the kind of man he wants to be (soft and warm)

instead of the kind a managerial "man" in his situation is expected to be (cold and hard). Because she is unable or unwilling to express the revolutionary feelings that she harbors, because she is unable or unwilling to "smash" the "sham" of it all, Clara, like Paul, adopts an outside self while trying to keep alive, simultaneously, an inside one. That is more than can be said for "Gyp," the girl who would gladly give up her true identity and language in exchange for the false, more "aristocratic" ones that she tries so desperately to learn. But it is also more painful to be a Clara or a Paul, for it is the tension between inward and outward roles that makes life so difficult for people like Gertrude and Walter, Paul and Miriam, Clara and Baxter Dawes. The tension, the difficulty, almost leaps off pages containing passages such as the following. "He himself," Lawrence writes of Paul in the chapter entitled "Passion," "seemed under a tight band of constraint."

> Then there was his other self, in the distance, doing things, entering stuff in a ledger, and he watched that far-off him carefully to see he made no mistake.
> But the ache and strain of it could not go on much longer. (305)

Lawrence focuses particularly on Jordan's factory in order to show how modern, industrial men and women are outwardly and inwardly divided by work that deforms them into machines and unsexed animals. The vision of mechanized man, however, is also to be found in those chapters devoted to Walter's work as a miner. When Lawrence refers to the military life, moreover, he returns to the same theme: modern work dehumanizes. "The *fool!*—the young fool!" Mrs. Morel cries when she first hears that Arthur has taken "the King's shilling" to join the army and that he now desperately wants out. "He'll look well in uniform," Paul responds "irritatingly":

> His mother turned on him like a fury.
> "Oh, will he!" she cried. "Not in my eyes! . . . a common soldier!"
> "Well," said Paul, "what am I but a common clerk?"

The Waste Land According to D. H. Lawrence

"A good deal, my boy!" cried his mother, stung.

"What?"

"At any rate, a *man*, and not a thing in a red coat."

"I shouldn't mind being in a red coat—or dark blue, that would suit me better—if they didn't boss me about too much." (181)

Lawrence is, of course, accomplishing several ends in the scene. One is to suggest, yet again, just how proud Gertrude Morel is and just how deeply she identifies with her son Paul. (Paul, once again, is associated slightly more with the color blue than with red, the color used in connection with Walter and Arthur.) She cannot stand the thought of commonness, especially the idea that Paul is common. At the same time, though, Lawrence would admit that Gertrude Morel is right: soldiering, exactly like manufacturing, takes a "man" and makes him into a "thing." If Paul is to be "a good deal more" than a thing, he will not become it while playing his clerk's role, and neither will Arthur become it by soldiering. "Just as he was getting on," Gertrude exclaims, ". . . here he goes and ruins himself for life. What good will he be . . . after *this?*"

"It may lick him into shape beautifully," said Paul.

"Lick him into shape!—lick what marrow there *was* out of his bones. A *soldier!*—a common *soldier!*—nothing but a body that makes movements when it hears a shout!" (181).

Again, Lawrence presents us with the idea of body without spirit or soul or intelligence. Again, one of Gertrude Morel's sons is threatened with becoming a mechanical man.

We have so far considered Lawrence's criticism, implied and explicit, of capitalist industrialism. Mining and manufacturing, however, are not the only institutions viewed critically in *Sons and Lovers*, nor are they the only institutions that, in Lawrence's view, have divided men and women within and without. Some of these other institutions, moreover, are traditions, and they have influenced English men and women far longer than Carston, Waite and Co. or Jordan's Surgical

Appliances. Lawrence particularly reflects on five of these traditional institutions: the class system, marriage, education, literature, and Christianity.

Unlike T. S. Eliot, Lawrence does not portray people divided by nationalities and languages; or, rather, he does not portray them in his first great novel, *Sons and Lovers*. He does, however, even in this early work, show people who are divided by class and by accent. Lily Western, better known as "Gyp," is a character through whom Lawrence expresses many of his attitudes toward the social class system and the stratification of speech forms that accompanies it. From the time William first brings the young woman home to meet his family, the Morels can tell from her clothes that she has a point to make: she is divided from them by social station. "[T]here was a chill in the atmosphere," Lawrence says with a double edge, when "Miss Western came down[stairs], having put on a purplish-coloured dress, very fine for the collier's kitchen" (116). The effect the dress has on Walter is to make him offer his seat close to the fire, and the interchange that follows his offer shows that language is as important as clothes in establishing class differences. "No, dad, keep your own chair," William insists, but to no avail:

> "No, no!" cried Morel. "This cheer's warmest. Come and sit here, Miss Wesson."
> "Thank you *so* much," said the girl, seating herself in the collier's arm-chair, the place of honour. . . .
> "Fetch me a hanky, Chubby dear!" she said, putting up her mouth to him, and using the same intimate tone as if they were alone; which made the rest of the family feel as if they ought not to be present. The young lady evidently did not realise them as people: they were creatures to her. (116–17)

The "rest of the family" is right. They are "to her . . . clownish—in short, the working classes" (117). And what is she to them?

To Walter Morel and the other children, Miss Western is cosmopolitan and refined: "She sat and talked about the dinner on the train, which had been so poor; about London, about dances. . . . Morel sat all the time smoking his thick twist tobacco, watching her, and listening to her glib London speech, as he puffed. . . . The three children sat round in silence and admiration. Miss Western was the princess" (117). William, too, sees her as something of a princess:

> At about ten o'clock he said to her:
> "Aren't you tired, Gyp?"
> "Rather, Chubby," she answered . . . putting her head slightly on one side.
> "I'll light her the candle, mother," he said. (117)

Gertrude Morel is less deferential to Miss Western, but even she has "dressed up in her best black silk blouse" and answered the young woman's questions "quietly and rather briefly" (117). Once again, clothes and manner of speech are intimately involved with class divisions. Gertrude dresses up and tones down her speech in recognition of Miss Western's apparent social superiority.

And an *apparent* social superiority it is. Miss Western is a fake, employing clothes and sophisticated diction in order to make people think she is something she is not. The morning after her arrival, she accompanies the Morel family to chapel, where

> She played the grand lady at first. When she went with William to chapel, he in his frock-coat and silk hat, she in her furs and London-made costume, Paul and Arthur and Annie expected everybody to bow to the ground in admiration. And Morel, standing in his Sunday suit. . . , felt he was the father of princes and princesses.
> And yet she was not so grand. For a year now she had been a sort of secretary or clerk in a London office. But while she was with the Morels she queened it. She sat and let Annie or Paul wait on her as if they were her servants. She treated Mrs. Morel with a certain glibness and Morel with patronage. But after a day or so she began to change her tune. (119)

Lawrence clearly shows, in passages like the one set forth above, how the social class system creates artificial barriers between people.

The values inherent in the system encourage a weak, vain, ambitious character such as Miss Western to mimic the clothes and speech of her "betters." By doing so, she hopes to distinguish herself from those into whose society she was born. In the process, of course, she divides herself not only from that community but also from the one into which she would enter, for its members inevitably recognize the falsity of the young woman's accent and usage. Finally, a self-division is created by the divisive class system, for Lily Western has to be two people: the person she is and the person she would be. She can play the latter role for an evening or even longer. Eventually, though, "after a day or so," the other self will show through and she will have "to change her tune." The need to be two people while social climbing is even suggested by the names Lawrence gives this character who is always either divided from society or from her own true nature. She requires both a name and a nickname, and a more incongruous pairing than "Gyp" and "Miss Lily Western" could hardly be imagined. "Gyp" suggests the gypsylike, ineducable darkness and wildness of a miner such as Walter Morel, while "Lily" suggests the purity and superiority of a Gertrude.

It is the prospect of marriage to the son of Gertrude and Walter, of course, that brings Miss Western and her airs to the Bottoms, and marriage, along with the class system with its various costumes and languages, is one of those institutions that create or at least exacerbate the inner and outer conflicts that Lawrence sees as being endemic to modern life. Just as society expects a man or a woman to play certain roles, whether or not those roles are natural to the individual concerned, so it expects every young person to marry, whether or not a suitable partner has been found, whether or not the individual is suited to meet the inevitable requirements of living with one of the opposite sex. *Sons and Lovers* is a novel inhabited by people who, like so many people in Lawrence's age: 1) married because they were expected to marry; 2) married without really knowing why they were marrying the person they were marrying; and 3) married the wrong person. "There were many, many stages in the ebbing of her love for him," Lawrence says, speaking of Gertrude Morel, "but it was always ebbing" (46). And yet the marriage remains in force, causing Gertrude to be what she less and less is, forcing her true nature to war more and more violently with the identity she assumed when she took her husband's name.

Lawrence focuses on four couples in order to suggest the divisive and damaging potential of the institution of marriage: Lily Western and William Morel, Gertrude and Walter Morel, Miriam and Paul, and Clara and Baxter Dawes. In William, he portrays a young man who really does not know why he is getting married. "[H]e discussed his sweetheart endlessly with his mother," we are told:

> "You know, mother, when I'm away from her I don't care for her a bit. I shouldn't care if I never saw her again. But, then, when I'm with her in the evenings I am awfully fond of her."
>
> "It's a queer sort of love to marry on," said Mrs. Morel, "if she holds you no more than that!"
>
> "It *is* funny!" he exclaimed. It worried and perplexed him. "But yet—there's so much between us now I couldn't give her up." (120)

William and Lily have nothing in common. Whereas "she never got beyond the second page" of a book, "he read a great deal, and had a quick, active intelligence. She could understand nothing but love-making and chatter" (131). When William is dominated by the "father" in him, he finds Lily an acceptable mate. When he is his mother, though, "he hate[s] his betrothed" (131). "It's a poor lookout," his mother warns him, and tells him he is making "a fine mess of a marriage." William becomes pale on hearing it, but he cannot seem to change his mind. He is kept from breaking free by two factors: his own physical, passional life, and social law or convention.

> He was pale, and his rugged face, that used to be so perfectly careless and laughing, was stamped with conflict and despair.
>
> "But I can't give her up now; it's gone too far," he said. "And besides, for *some* things I couldn't do without her. (131)

Just as part of his mother needs her husband, so part of William finds satisfaction with Lily. Another part—his "quick, active intelligence"—does not, but that is the very part of him that understands morality, sees the sense of rules, and respects commitments. And the rule is that a man, having made love to a woman, had better go on with wedding plans. William happens to be "saved" from the disastrous marriage that social convention would dictate, from the division and self-loathing that would follow the wedding as inevitably as they followed his own parents' wedding. He is, to be sure, tragically saved—by illness and death. Still, it may be that physical death is less horrible than the kind his mother had warned him about. "My boy, remember you're taking your life in your hands," she had said, on hearing him say that "for *some* things" he "couldn't do without" Gyp. "*Nothing* is as bad as a marriage that's a hopeless failure" (132).

As these passages make clear, the division that exists between William's active intelligence and his equally active sexual identity may ultimately be natural, part of his makeup. Thus, to some extent, the division that spells doom for his relationship with Lily is also natural. It is not society, after all, that gave him enough intelligence to grow frustrated at times with this girl who "could understand nothing but love-making and chatter." But neither is it clear that, were it not for the class system, Lily would ever have been attracted to an intelligent, avid reader working as a clerk in a lawyer's office. And it seems especially unlikely that, were it not for the institution of marriage, William would have ever considered binding himself permanently to Gyp.

Thus society, though it may not entirely create the novel's inward and outer conflicts, makes them horribly worse by threatening to institutionalize them, thereby making permanent problems that might otherwise have been passing ones. "I think she's dissatisfied," Miriam says of Clara Dawes, who is separated from her husband. "What with?" Paul responds by asking.

> "Well—how would *you* like to be tied for life to a man like that?"
> "Why did she marry him, then, if she was to have revulsions so soon?"
> "Ay, why did she!" repeated Miriam bitterly. (187)

Miriam, down deep, knows why Clara married. She knows that Clara has a powerful physical identity that responded to Baxter's. Consequently, social convention dictated their marriage. She married for the same reason William almost did, and the revulsion of her other nature, her "active intelligence," is the very same revulsion that William was beginning to feel, even before going to the altar. Indeed, the story of Clara and Baxter carries on, late in the novel, the story of William and Lily that is cut short early in the book by the death of William. "Did you love him when you married him?" Paul asks Clara in chapter 10. "I thought I did—more or less," she answers. "I didn't think much about it. And he wanted me. I was very prudish then" (274). Clara only wanted Baxter physically, but she knows the social convention. If she is to have him, she is to marry him and live with him forever.

In dealing with the Miriam-Paul relationship, Lawrence looks at the other side of what society expects marriage to be. On one hand, convention dictates that physical passion, where it exists and is being acted upon, be legitimated in marriage, even if those passions are little more than a passing fancy. On the other hand, conventional "wisdom" has it that marriage is not really the place for passion, and that a young man or woman should, if at all possible, marry for "higher" reasons. Neither Miriam nor Clara is right for Paul, and yet Paul feels a social pressure both 1) to marry and 2) to marry a certain kind of mate, that is, one that satisfies one of his two selves—but not the other. Paul "loved Miriam with his soul," whereas "he grew warm at the thought of Clara, . . . knew the curves of her breast and shoulders as if they had been moulded inside him. . . . He believed himself really bound to Miriam. If ever he should marry, some time in the far future, it would be his *duty* to marry Miriam. That he gave Clara to understand, and she said nothing" (276, italics mine). Again, Lawrence shows how tragic marriages come about because of feelings of duty that are socially induced.

It is difficult to know with certainty whether or not Lawrence believes that certain social institutions have actually created the internal split in an individual like Paul. Perhaps they have—but perhaps they have not—brought about the internal divorce of the side that loves by "growing warm" from the side that wishes for cooler, more intellectual comradeship. One thing, though, we can be certain of: Society, which may or may not create the conflict in Paul that causes his problems with Miriam and Clara, threatens to make those divisions worse by eternizing them. Social conventions, which may or may not bring about Gertrude Morel's desire to learn theology or Miriam Leivers's insistence on being learned, turn those desires and wishes into painful forces by defining them as unquenchable, thus frustrating them. As a result, they are turned into forces that can only do damage—externally but also internally. The theologian in Gertrude has nothing better to do than feel jealousy and hatred toward the soft sensualist in Gertrude, the side of the woman that is deemed appropriate and legitimate and that is allowed expression, even though it is the weaker, less characteristic side of her identity.

Thus, although society did not create the division of humankind into two genders, it seems to have contributed to the battle between the sexes, and it has undeniably turned that battle into a war. Instead of simply recognizing the different physical capabilities and needs of males and females, society has created arbitrary divisions that effectively separate the economic and domestic spheres, wives from the former, husbands from the latter. Gertrude, who has more of a head for money than her husband, is, according to custom, kept in the dark about what she owes and owns (12–13). Her money—if she has any—is what is left over after her husband has drunk his fill, and it is to be spent on the family. Moreover, if he takes what little money that has been left to her out of her purse, she can do little about it but verbally object and suffer a consequent beating. Thus Lawrence describes, in *Sons and Lovers*, a much poorer class of people than the miners who risk their lives daily in the holes in the ground owned by Carston, Waite and Co. Women are the poorest of the poor. There are no Robin Hoods on the scene, moreover, who are in a position to come to their rescue—unless they are those men who, like Paul, redistribute to the female world some small parcel of that knowledge with which the male world is rich.

The division of men from women caused by the association of men with learning and women with feeling turns out to be incremental, for the division of women from learning causes women to hate men. "Miriam almost fiercely wished she were a man. And yet she hated men at the same time." This hatred, certainly, is not natural. It is induced by an arbitrary and unjust social order the arbitrariness of which men are virtually unaware.

> "But it's as well to be a woman as a man," [Paul] said, frowning.
> "Ha! Is it? Men have everything."
> "I should think women ought to be as glad to be women as men are to be men," he answered.
> "No!"—she shook her head— "no! Everything the men have."
> "But what do you want?" he asked.
> "I want to learn. Why *should* it be that I know nothing?"
> "What! such as mathematics and French?"
> "Why *shouldn't* I know mathematics? Yes!" she cried, her eye expanding in a kind of defiance.
> "Well, you can learn as much as I know," he said. "I'll teach you, if you like." (154–55)

In the moment Paul agrees to teach Miriam what he knows, he narrows somewhat the division between men and women that society has created. He is unusual, though, in doing so, and when he actually begins teaching Miriam, he vacillates back and forth between his "Robin Hood" identity and a more conventional male identity. "He was always either in a rage or very gentle" in teaching her (156).

Much of what Paul teaches Miriam, moreover, is literature, and literature is itself embedded with the arbitrary values held by society. Through Paul, Miriam deepens her understanding of literature, but literature is a social institution just like marriage. Like marriage, moreover, literature has its rules, proprieties, and conventions. Thus, in a sense, Miriam cannot win for losing, for when she decides to rise above the role that patriarchal society has designed for women, she must learn, but what she learns confirms, even if only subtly, the patriarchal value system.

The particular kind of literature Miriam reads, moreover, exacerbates the problem of the divided self, or the self in conflict with self, by encouraging the imagination to sustain a fictional self and a set of impossible expectations that are bound to be at odds with those that the reality-bound self may afford to entertain. Indeed, we might even say that the kind of romance beloved of Miriam creates two false selves, for it gets its reader not only to think of herself as, potentially, a princess, but also to think of herself in the meantime as something lower, more degraded, than she really is. (Miriam sees herself, through other people's eyes, as a "swine girl" or "beggar's maid" in "rags," whereas what she really looks like is a well-cared-for farmer's daughter.) Once again, we cannot say that, without the inspiration of romantic poems and novels by Scott, Miriam would not naturally tend to imagine herself living other, more uncommon existences. Lawrence says quite clearly that, "like her mother," Miriam was "inclined to be mystical," which would seem to imply that her mind is, by its nature, prone to dream dreams and think far-off thoughts. But were it not for the fairy-tale romance tradition, would she imagine that there is "a princess beneath" the skin of what looks like a "swine girl"? Would she so "hate . . . her position" as a farmer's daughter if she were not always reading highly fanciful romances about maidens regularly released from their "bondage," their "beggars' . . . rags," to assume their rightful places at the sides of "Walter Scott hero[es]"? Would she expect, moreover, to find a love that is nothing less than the "soul union" portrayed by a poet such as Shelley (277)? Shelley, who wrote shortly after Wordsworth, spoke in his "Epipsychidion" of lover's love as if it made "one / Spirit within two frames," which "grows . . ."

> Till like two meteors of expanding flame,
> Those spheres instinct with it become the same,
> Touch, mingle, are transfigured; ever still
> Burning, yet ever inconsumable. (ll. 573–79)

Similarly, Miriam might naturally experience nature as a "mystery," but without Wordsworth to "nourish . . . her heart," would she think of evening as a "pure" and "holy" nun and, therefore, "like herself"?

Obviously, Lawrence can hardly afford to be "against" literature;

however anti-institutional a writer he may be, he participates in the traditions of novel writing and alludes to the poets of the past. What he is, rather, is critical of a certain kind of literature, namely, that which gets us to think in terms of the far-off and unavailable and which, at the same time, denigrates all that is common, earthy, earthly, and available to enjoy. The literature that exacerbates self-division and feelings of alienation from the human and natural world is romantic, idealistic literature, a tradition of literature that includes the novels of Scott, the poetry of Wordsworth, Shelley, and Tennyson, and, of course, the Bible.

The Bible is, after all, not only yet another text that speaks to the "mystical" nature but also the text of the Judeo-Christian religious heritage, yet another tradition that, though it may not cause every conflict and instance of self-division described by the novel, intensifies those inner and outer tensions. Miriam, Lawrence says in the "Lad-and-Girl Love" chapter, "was cut off from ordinary life by her religious intensity which made the world for her either a nunnery garden or a paradise, where sin and knowledge were not, or else an ugly, cruel thing" (148). A religion such as Miriam's, then, like poetry such as Wordsworth's, cuts its devotee off from reality by putting him or her in touch with a nature that, in Lawrence's view, does not exist except in the fictions spun by the human imagination. In addition to cutting Miriam off from natural reality, moreover, her brand of religion cuts her off from other men and women. It contributes to, if it does not actually cause, her initial aversion to lovemaking, and it unquestionably hinders her from enjoying physical contact *as* physical contact, once she finally succumbs to Paul's overtures. In the moment in which she acquiesces in Paul's wish to have sex, she prays, "But, Lord, if it is Thy will that I should love him, make me love him—as Christ would, who died for the souls of men."

> "Make me love him splendidly, because he is Thy son."
> She remained kneeling for some time, quite still, and deeply moved. . . . Then she fell into that rapture of self-sacrifice, identifying herself with a God who was sacrificed, which gives to so many human souls their deepest bliss. (172)

Miriam's religion, by dividing her off from nature and by hindering her sexual enjoyment of another, also divides her within, for the awareness of sex as self-sacrifice, indeed, the very concept of self-sacrifice, entails a kind of self-division. When a person says, or even thinks, a thought such as "this is my body, given for you"—whether that person be Jesus Christ speaking at the Last Supper or Miriam Leivers speaking to Paul Morel—that person is withdrawing in mind and spirit from the bodily self, conceiving of the physical existence as the other, as something apart from mental or spiritual consciousness.

7

MODERN DIVISION AS EPIDEMIC DISEASE
Fire Baptism as Individual Cure

We have seen how Lawrence suggests that certain fundamental social institutions worsen, if they do not actually cause, the inner and outer conflicts that are described by *Sons and Lovers*. The tensions produced within Paul and between Gertrude and Walter Morel by the attraction of mother to son, and vice versa, offer a case in point. Perhaps the powerful love that Paul and his mother feel for one another springs from characteristics encoded in their natures. Perhaps these fundamentally biological characteristics make possible that romantic, at times almost sexual, attraction that Freud used the word *Oedipal* to describe. If we remember the story of Oedipus, however, we will recall that even the original Oedipal relationship was engendered by a complex interplay of forces and authorities outside of and beyond those at work within the bodies and families of the victims. (Had mother and son been in a position to recognize one another as relations, would the tragic attraction have even developed?) Similarly, with respect to Lawrence's latter-day family romance, we can hardly fail to observe that it is society—not biology—that says working and supporting a family economically are things husbands, not wives, do. Gertrude Morel has a husband who cannot seem to play those roles but a son who can and does. As a child, Paul picks up his father's checks; as a teenager he wins cash prizes for his art; as a young man he begins working at a job and earning income that supports the family. By society's definition, Paul is, from childhood on, a better "husband" than his father is. Is it any wonder that he seems, at times, as much his mother's lover as her son?

If society causes some of the conflicts that exist within and between the paired characters we have studied, and if it does not cause but does exacerbate some of the others, can society mend the divisions and self-divisions? That is to say, can institutions be modified into—or swept away and replaced by—new institutions and traditions that will heal the breaches between male and female, body and spirit, intelligence and instinct, brain and blood consciousness that cause modern individuals so much pain? Lawrence raises the question, in part, simply by writing a novel that is conscious of the role literature plays in cutting certain people off from reality and from their own true identities. By contrasting Miriam's love of Wordsworth and Scott with her dislike of two French poets, Lawrence suggests that there are literary alternatives to the idealistic, romantic poetry that intrudes between Miriam and Paul, Miriam and her body, Miriam and nature, Miriam and her social identity. Could an alternative literature heal rather than widen the breaches between—and within—men and women?

In an essay entitled "Poetry of the Present," published in 1918 as the introduction to *New Poems,* five years after the publication of *Sons and Lovers,* Lawrence defines idealistic, romantic poetry as "the poetry of perfection." He uses Keats and Shelley rather than Wordsworth, this time, as examples of the kind of literature that should be abandoned: "Perfected bygone moments, perfected moments in the glimmering futurity, these are the treasured gem-like lyrics of Shelley and Keats." Lawrence next applauds, by contrast, a poetry begun by Whitman that captures "the immediate present" instead of making us sigh for what is not:

> In the immediate present there is no perfection, no consummation, nothing finished. The strands are all flying, quivering, intermingling

into the web. . . . There is poetry of this immediate present, instant poetry, as well as poetry of the infinite past and the infinite future. The seething poetry of the incarnate Now is supreme, beyond even the everlasting gems of the before and after. . . . Whitman truly looked before and after. But he did not sigh for what is not. The clue to all his utterance lies in the sheer appreciation of the instant moment, life surging itself into utterance at its very well-head.[56]

If such a poetry becomes a literary institution, then the institution of literature might cease to promote and even begin to heal breaches between soul and body, male and female, man and nature as it really is. By writing *Sons and Lovers,* of course, Lawrence is writing such a work of literature, an example of what he might have called "the Fiction of the Present."

In addition to suggesting that literary tradition might, if revised, contribute less to the consciousness and self-consciousness that cut us off from ourselves, one another, and "the incarnate Now," Lawrence alludes to the feminism of his day. He can hardly afford to ignore the movement to liberate women, given the fact that much of the pain suffered by characters in the novel is defined by sex roles prescribed within the economic, industrial, educational, and marital institutions. Might feminism be part of the cure for the disease of modern life?

In Lawrence's view, the answer seems to be no. This is not to say that Lawrence is insensitive to the frustrations felt by women; indeed, although modern feminist critics sometimes decry his male chauvinism, they do so to a great extent because he foregrounds feminist issues, rather than simply ignoring them as did many of the writers of his day. In addressing those issues, he demonstrates a consciousness far ahead of its time—but not so far advanced as the consciousness of feminist critics, male or female, writing today. The passage below demonstrates both Lawrence's awareness of feminist attitudes and his ambivalence toward them, for in it Lawrence makes Paul seem offensively provocative on the one hand while seeming, in some sense, reasonable and right on the other. "You were at Margaret Bonford's meeting the other evening," Paul says to Clara in Miriam's presence, referring to a women's rights advocate of the day:

"Yes," she said.

"Why," asked Miriam, "how do you know?"

"I went in for a few minutes before the train came," he answered. . . . "I think she's a lovable little woman. . . ."

"Margaret Bonford!" exclaimed Clara. "She's a great deal cleverer than most men."

"Well, I didn't say she wasn't," he said, deprecating. "She's lovable for all that."

"And, of course, that is all that matters," said Clara witheringly.

He rubbed his head, rather perplexed, rather annoyed.

"I suppose it matters more than her cleverness," he said; "which, after all, would never get her to heaven."

"It's not heaven she wants to get—it's her fair share on earth," retorted Clara. She spoke as if he were responsible for some deprivation which Miss Bonford suffered.

"Well," he said, "I thought she was warm, and awfully nice—only too frail. I wished she was sitting comfortably in peace—"

" 'Darning her husband's stockings,' " said Clara scathingly.

" I'm sure she wouldn't mind darning even my stockings," he said. . . . "Just as I wouldn't mind blacking her boots if she wanted me to." (230–31)

Paul is offensive in calling Margaret Bonford "a lovable little woman," in suggesting that her cleverness will not get her to heaven, and in wishing her home in a comfortable chair. Clara is right to suggest that what he really wishes is that she would stick to darning men's socks and stop rocking the boat. Paul is, here, speaking as a conventional "man," being the pious, chauvinistic self that his society has taught him to be. On the other hand, there is more in the passage than just criticism of Paul's narrowness. There is the countersuggestion that feminism, which seeks to end divisions between men and women, creates them as fast as it eliminates them. (Clara is "deprecating," "withering," "scathing.") More important, the passage quietly suggests that feminism causes women to reject certain roles and identities that need not be ridiculed and rejected even as it makes it possible for them to be selves and play roles that have up to now been forbidden. There may be nothing wrong with a woman being "lovable" or with her darning a lover's stockings, for that matter, while her lover blackens her boots. By causing women to reject conventional roles and identities to make clear a point about the need for freedom and equality, feminism, in Lawrence's view, only encourages them to exchange one half of a life or self for another. Feminism cannot heal the divisions and self-divisions depicted in *Sons and Lovers* until it can allow the coexistence of a woman's clever and lovable, independent and helpful, political and sensual, selves. Until then, it will be an intellectual movement that, like all such movements, including romantic ideology, discourages instinct and sensuality as powerfully as patriarchal chauvinism has discouraged the development of women's intellect. So goes Lawrence's implied, admittedly chauvinistic, argument.

Lawrence not only suggests that feminism will take a long while to heal more divisions than it causes, but he also implies that feminists, like all human beings, are complex and self-divided. Thus they are prone to self-conflict, to undermining their own efforts. Even while there are men, worse than Paul, resisting the changes that would allow women like Miriam or Gertrude to be unapologetically clever, there are also counterforces and feelings within feminist women themselves. Once again, Lawrence stops short of saying whether or not these counterforces, counterfeelings, are natural: they may be induced by the chauvinistic society. They are, however, there. If they were not, Clara Dawes and her mother would not struggle to make it economically on their own by going into the cottage industry of lace making. Lawrence has deliberately chosen lace for its symbolic value; it is a commodity inextricably involved with the prefeminist view of women as pure, delicate, and attractively flimsy. By having the intellectual, feminist Clara make a living by manufacturing lace, Lawrence makes her into something of a contradiction. He does not say whether the contradiction is forced upon her by economic realities or chosen freely by her in the complexity of her nature. He does suggest, though, that there is a side of her—the side that was once attracted to Baxter Dawes—that continues to exist and that may never cooperate with its aspiring and militant alter ego.

The story of the Dawes couple is an important one, even though Clara and Baxter may seem, at first, to be relatively minor characters.

Through them, Lawrence repeats and develops many of the ideas and images he has explored while writing about Paul and Miriam, Gertrude and Walter.

Clara, of course, completes a triangle of which Paul and Miriam are the other two corners. That triangle is significant, for it repeats, roughly, the triangular structure that Lawrence uses in depicting the relationship between Paul, his father, and his mother. As we have seen, Walter Morel is mainly a sensual, nonintellectual character; his wife is a highly conscious, intellectual, and moral person; and their son Paul has both natures warring within him. At times he is inclined toward his mother's corner of the triangle, but at other times toward his father's directly opposite side. And, of course, Paul is involved in a similar, triangular relationship with Miriam and Clara, for whereas Miriam is almost all soul, purity, and intellect (she is associated, as Gertrude Morel is, with the colors white and blue), Clara is overbalanced on the sensual, animal side of her nature. Paul is alternately pulled in the direction of one woman, then the other; conflict between the two women, like the conflict between his mother and father, is more or less an outward duplication of a conflict that goes on inside him.

Because Clara is the more sensual, physical, and unconscious of the two women, we are not surprised to find her associated with Walter Morel's colors. One of those colors is, of course, red. One day, after the two have met at "the Fountain," after work, Paul walks Clara to a florist's and buys her "a bunch of scarlet, brick-red carnations," which "[s]he put . . . in her coat, flushing" (305). After that, they take a walk to the Castle rock, enter the Grove, climb down a red clay bank to the riverside, and make love for the first time. Finally, they have tea in the house of an old woman who probably suspects what they have been doing and who seems to find them attractive for having done it. She offers Clara radishes from her garden and, when Clara accepts, picks the young woman not only radishes but also "dahlias . . . speckled scarlet and white" (312–13). As a result of the afternoon's lovemaking, Paul decides he wants his mother to meet Clara, who agrees to come on a Sunday afternoon. He meets her at the train station and walks her home past hedgerows he cannot pass up: "They took the road into Nuttall and over the Reckoning House Farm. . . . Everywhere the brown leaves lay scattered; many scarlet hips stood upon the hedge beside the wood. He gathered a few for her to wear" (319).

Like Walter Morel, too, Clara is associated not only with redness but also with fire. She and Paul make love one evening in the house that Clara shares with her mother. Paul, who has gone up to bed first, returns to the kitchen after old Mrs. Radford has gone to bed. He hopes to find Clara still there, and when he shuts the kitchen door "noisily behind him" so that the "old woman daren't come" and snoop on her daughter, he is not disappointed: "Then he stood, arrested. Clara was kneeling on a pile of white underclothing on the hearth-rug, her back towards him, warming herself. She did not look round, but sat crouching on her heels, and her rounded beautiful back was towards him, and her face was hidden. She was warming her body at the fire for consolation. The glow was rosy on one side, the shadow dark and warm on the other" (338). The passage, like several devoted to Walter Morel, is the only one in which Lawrence associates Clara with warmth, fire, redness, and darkness, all at the same time. Again and again, though, he returns to the idea of warmth and fire—as well as to red and "shadow[y]" colors—in order to suggest both the physicality of her nature and the nature of physical passion. "And after such an evening they both were very still, having known the immensity of passion," Lawrence writes in a later chapter. A page later he says that

> When she saw him that day at the factory her heart melted like a drop of fire. It was his body, his brows. The drop of fire grew more intense in her breast; she must hold him. . . . She followed him into the dark, ugly basement, and lifted her arms to him. He kissed her, and the intensity of passion began to burn him again. . . .
> After that the fire slowly went down. He felt more and more that his experience had been impersonal, and not Clara. He loved her . . . but it was not she who could keep his soul steady. (354–55)

When she is not associated with fire, "scarlet," "red," "vermilion" (305), moreover, Clara is associated with the "dusky, golden softness" that is used to characterize Walter. At one point, while she sits "leaning on [a] table," Paul notices the "fine golden hairs" on the skin of her arms (230). Such moments fill him, typically, with physical desire that he cannot seem to control, that indeed seems to take control of his conscious mind. One such moment is described in the "Passion" chapter. Paul has taken Clara to the Theatre Royal in Nottingham, to watch Sarah Bernhardt perform *La Dame aux Camélias*. Once again, Paul's physical passion is aroused by Clara's arms and hands; once again, Lawrence makes the connection between Clara, fire, and the redness of passion. This time, though, he does it subtly through a reference to blood. He suggests that Clara's "beauty . . . torture[s]" Paul by bringing his blood to the boiling point:

> [H]e loved her as she balanced her head and stared straight in front of her, pouting, wistful, immobile. . . . A kind of eternal look about her, as if she were a wistful sphinx, made it necessary to him to kiss her. He dropped his [play] programme, and crouched down on the floor to get it, so that he could kiss her hand and wrist. . . . [W]hen the lights went down, she sank a little against him, and he caressed her hand and arm with his fingers. He could smell her faint perfume. All the time his blood kept sweeping up in great white-hot waves that killed his consciousness momentarily. (331)

Like Morel, Clara has little use for rules that would limit her freedom. Unlike Miriam, the woman Paul's soul cries out for, Clara has an outwardly "defiant" spirit about her, and Paul tells his mother that he likes her for her defiant, often "angry way" (242). Elsewhere Lawrence depicts Clara as an Amazon, thus reinforcing both our image of her as a defiant woman and our sense that she is predominantly physical, not soulful or intellectual, by nature. The scene is one in which Paul, Clara, Miriam, and her brothers are sporting in a field; everyone save Miriam is jumping hay bales for fun. "Miriam did not care for the game, and stood aside. Edgar and Geoffrey and Maurice and Clara and Paul jumped. Paul won, because he was light. Clara's blood was roused. She could run like an Amazon. Paul loved the determined way she rushed at the haycock and leaped, landed on the other side, her breasts shaken, her thick hair come undone" (250). Once again, Lawrence connects the determined and defiant, "Amazonian" Clara not only with passion but also with the redness of blood.

Although the father in Paul is attracted to Clara, the mother in him wants someone quite different and soulful. Thus, part of Paul is dissatisfied, making him want Clara "to be something she could not be" (355). Part of him, though, is delighted by what Clara is, and as a result Paul finds himself loving and hating Clara alternately—sometimes even simultaneously: "Something in him hated her again for submitting him to this torture of nearness. And he loved her as she balanced her head and stared straight in front of her" (331). Because of his own self-division, Paul can neither love—nor satisfy—Clara completely. Indeed, Lawrence suggests that Clara stays with Paul as long as she does because she wants satisfaction from a man and "he never satisfied her" (355). At one point "a flash of hate for her" is felt by Paul when he realizes that "she was dissatisfied with him, even there, where he thought they fulfilled each other." Lawrence immediately suggests, though, that what dissatisfies Clara is not any physical failure as a lover on Paul's part. It is, rather, the feeling she gets when she makes love to him, the feeling that she is getting only half of him.

> "I feel," she continued slowly, "as if I hadn't got you, as if all of you weren't there, and as if it weren't *me* you were taking. . . . When I had Baxter, actually had him, then I *did* feel as if I had all of him," she said.
>
> "And it was better?" he asked.
>
> "Yes, yes; it was more whole. I don't say you haven't given me more than he ever gave me."
>
> "Or could give you."
>
> "Yes, perhaps; but you've never given me yourself." (363)

Baxter, Clara's estranged husband, was able to give himself more completely to Clara because his identity is not as divided as Paul's. Whereas Clara's sensuousness elicits a positive response from one side of Paul's nature and a negative one from the side that is "steadied" by Miriam, it elicits a far more unified, approving response from the less self-conflicted Baxter.

Paul and Clara discuss her relationship with Baxter at several points. Those discussions help lead Clara back to the man who, though relatively limited in what he could offer and relatively uncomplicated by nature, could at least give himself wholeheartedly. They help Clara to see, for one thing, that just as she cannot completely satisfy Paul, so she cannot completely know him, for the side of him that "hates" her is never interested in drawing close to her. She admits at one point that she never knew Baxter much better than she knows Paul, but she also admits that that may have been partly her own fault. "[Y]ou've never come near to me," she says to Paul at one point.

> "You can't come out of yourself, you can't. Baxter could do that better than you."
> [Paul] walked on pondering. He was angry with her for preferring Baxter to him.
> "You begin to value Baxter now . . ." he said. (362)

In discussing the Daweses and Paul's relationship to them, of course, we must be careful about oversimplifying the facts. For one thing, if Clara were as sensual and instinctual as Miriam is soulful and intellectual, then she would not, presumably, have come to resent her husband in the way that Gertrude Morel came to resent hers, and she would certainly not have separated from him. The fact that she has—and that she attends meetings devoted to women's rights and addressed by feminists such as Margaret Bonford—suggests that her personality has several different facets. When we recall that even Miriam has a sensual side to her character, we should not be surprised to find that Clara, too, has some inward complexity. Paul may be right to think that her nature is, generally speaking, physical and sensual, but he distorts the facts quite unfairly when he accuses her of "always want[ing] to be kissing and embracing" (355). He must realize, moreover, that he distorts the facts, for he knows, even before he meets Clara, that she is "supposed to be clever," and cleverness is part of what has "interested" him in her since the early days of their relationship. If we recall the dahlias given to Clara by the old woman at whose house the lovers have tea, and if we recall Lawrence's symbolic use of flowers in the novel, we will remember that they were scarlet *and* white. In other words, we will realize that Lawrence was countering, with them, our tendency to oversimplify the character of this, the novel's most sexually liberated woman.

On the other hand, if Clara is a complex character, containing a "red" but also a "white" nature, a tendency to abandon herself to a lover who abandons himself to her but also a tendency to feel proud and independent, then why does her relationship with Paul fail, and why does she go back to her relatively uncomplicated husband? For she does go back to him; indeed, she decides she has been "vile" to him and even that she "*made* him horrid" while "he loved [her] a thousand times better than [Paul] ever did" (383). Let us assume, for a moment, that Lawrence thinks of Paul, Baxter, and Clara as forming yet another triangle, one involving two rivals, Baxter and Paul—who are unalike in that the former is simple by nature, the latter complex— and a woman torn between them. If Clara turns out to be complex like Paul, should not the triangle be broken by Clara's turn to Paul and not by her return to Baxter?

There is no simple interpretation of Lawrence's final disposition of the characters in the novel; indeed, there is no simple answer to any of the questions that have plagued interpreters of the final chapters of the book. The reasons for Clara's return to Baxter—besides those that are grounded in biographical facts that could have been changed by the novelist—are all as debatable as is the tone of the novel's final paragraph. Be that as it may, let us venture some speculative explanations for Clara's return to Baxter, not all of which are consistent.

For one thing, and as we have already discovered, characters in *Sons and Lovers* are complicated or uncomplicated by degrees. Even simple men and women are double and even duplicitous in the pejorative sense by nature: that is one of the radical meanings the novel has to offer. That does not mean, however, that Miriam or Walter—or Clara—is as self-divided as Paul. If Clara becomes comfortable with her own contradiction, then she may come to have more in common with her relatively uncontradicted husband than she does with her young friend, who loves and hates her in the very same moment.

And Baxter is a relatively unself-contradicted man. He is, pre-dominantly and rather simply, a sensualist, an unambiguous, "dark" character in the mold of Walter Morel: "His hair was of soft brown, his moustache was golden. . . . His eyes, dark brown and quick-shift-ing, were dissolute. They protruded very slightly, and his eyelids hung over them. . . . His mouth, too, was sensual. His whole manner was of cowed defiance, as if he were ready to knock anybody down who disapproved of him—perhaps because he really disapproved of him-self" (185). Not only is Baxter associated with darkness, soft gold (his skin, like his mustache, is said to have a "golden tinge"), and sensual-ity, but he is also associated with furious, reckless behavior, and with the redness of fire (185). His vocation, indeed, is that of blacksmith, one of Walter Morel's avocations.

Given the bitter conflict between Paul and his father, we are hardly surprised to learn, in the relatively early "Strife in Love" chap-ter, that

> From the first day [Baxter] had hated Paul. Finding the lad's imper-sonal, deliberate gaze of an artist on his face, he got into a fury.
> "What are yer lookin' at?" he sneered, bullying.
> The boy glanced away. But the smith used to stand behind the counter and talk to Mr. Pappleworth. His speech was dirty, with a kind of rottenness. Again he found the youth with his cool, critical gaze fixed on his face. The smith started round as if he had been stung. (186)

Once again, Lawrence pairs characters with doubles on the one hand and with opposites on the other. Baxter is as hot, dark, uncontrolled, and dirty as Walter was; Paul is cool, clean, impersonal and deliberate. Because the two are so different, "Paul and he were confirmed ene-mies" (341), "rival men" doomed to "f[ight]" all the time (379), po-tentially "deadly rivals," in fact, opposites that Clara is being asked to choose between (384). "[T]he two never looked at each other save in hostility" (341).

If Baxter were purely savage, sensual, and instinctual, however, he would be an exception to the rule in *Sons and Lovers*. That is to say, he would contradict the suggestion implied by all the other characters in the novel, namely, that all individuals have two sides or selves. When we begin examining passages closely, moreover, when we begin looking at all the evidence, even in the passages quoted above, we discover that Dawes is not such an exception, after all. In the very passages in which he most looks like the elder Mr. Morel, Lawrence allows us glimpses of another side of Baxter's nature, a side or a self able to criticize his own, dominant nature. He looks "as if he were ready to knock anybody down who disapproved of him," Lawrence says, "—perhaps because he really disapproved of himself" (185).

Thus, somewhere inside him, there is a self that does not like the dominant self. That critical self is not enemy to, hostile toward, or the rival of, Paul. Indeed, the very sentences that are used above to show the fundamental opposition between the two men have been taken from passages that, when considered in their entirety, reveal a subtler but nonetheless real affinity, too: "Paul and he were confirmed enemies, and yet there was between them that peculiar feeling of intimacy, as if they were secretly near to each other, which sometimes exists between two people, although they never speak to one another. Paul often thought of Baxter Dawes, often wanted to get at him and be friends with him. He knew that Dawes often thought about him, and that the man was drawn to him by some bond or other. And yet the two never looked at each other save in hostility" (341). "There was a feeling of connection between the rival men, more than ever since they had fought," Lawrence comments in the chapter that follows the one in which Baxter beats and kicks Paul, dislocating his shoulder in the process. When Paul goes to Sheffield to see his mother, who is suffering from the cancerous tumor that will eventually kill her, he discovers that Baxter is in the "fever hospital" there, suffering from typhoid fever. He consequently goes "to see Dawes once or twice. There was a sort of friendship between the two men, who were all the while deadly rivals" (384).

The feeling of connection, of course, does not by itself prove that

Dawes has two natures, or two sides to his nature. We know, after all, that Paul has his father in him as well as his mother; thus, we might argue, there is a nature inside Paul that corresponds to Baxter Dawes's simple, single nature. There is reason to think, though, that Baxter is not as simple as he seems. For one thing, there are passages like the one above in which Baxter stands outside his usual self and examines it critically. For another, there is the fact that illness brings out a different Baxter Dawes, one who finds it easier to relate to the artistic, conscious, intellectual Paul. Finally, and most obviously, the Baxter that "from the first day . . . had hated Paul" is not the same one that "often thought about [Paul], and . . . was drawn to him by some bond or other."

Baxter thus is more complicated than he seems—than society encourages him to be outwardly. Thus, Clara may be torn between two self-conflicted men, one of whom (Baxter) is self-conflicted more in the way that, and to the degree that, she herself is.

If new traditions within society—new traditions of poetry, new traditions such as women's rights—cannot bridge the gaps between alienated selves, cannot end the feelings of self-alienation that Eliot describes in "The Love Song of J. Alfred Prufrock" and that Lawrence affirms in his fiction, then what can bring a healing end to the modern angst, the modern condition? What, in Eliot's terms, can rejuvenate the twentieth-century wasteland, or can it be rejuvenated? Many students of Eliot find little hope in *The Waste Land* itself and believe that Eliot only found reason for optimism after his conversion to Christianity. Does Lawrence, who never underwent a similarly powerful conversion to conventional religious faith, see any hope that his England of symbolically drab houses, dusty black mines, and smouldering ash pits will become once again the Merry Old England of yore? Can the world of Robin Hood be resurrected?

Lawrence is an artist—not a sociologist, psychologist, or philosopher, and so he offers an answer that is more beautiful than definite or prescriptive. Besides, *Sons and Lovers* is the early work of a young artist whose ideas are not final or settled. Still, Lawrence does seem to find something positive to build on in the world he describes, and in his later novels he develops that something into a positive antidote to the sickness that pervades modern life.

The antidote he prescribes is not to be found in old, revised, or entirely new social structures, institutions, or traditions. Humanity will resurrect itself on an individual, not a group, basis. Individuals will heal themselves through relationships with other individuals, but self-saved souls will emerge from those relationships with their integrity and individuality intact. If such relationships can take place within the confines of marriage, then marriage as an institution can be reformed and will no longer be a source of conflict between and self-conflict within husband and wife. But marriage will not itself be the cure. Rather, a certain kind of relationship that can be nurtured inside or outside marriage will be.

Lawrence most clearly expresses this theory of a healing relationship between distinct individuals in the "Passion" chapter that we have just examined, the chapter devoted mainly to Paul's relationship with Clara and Baxter Dawes. Miriam, of course, figures in that chapter, too; in it, she and Paul approach an understanding of what has been wrong with their relationship. One day, "when [Paul] saw Miriam, the conversation turned to marriage, then to Clara's marriage with Dawes":

> "You see," he said, "she never knew the fearful importance of marriage. She thought it was all in the day's march—it would have to come—and Dawes—well, a good many women would have given their souls to get him; so why not him? . . ."
>
> "And she left him because he didn't understand her?"
>
> ". . . I suppose she had to. It isn't altogether a question of understanding; it's a question of living. With him, she was only half-alive; the rest was dormant, deadened. . . ."
>
> "And what about him."
>
> "I don't know. I rather think he loves her as much as he can, but he's a fool." (316–17)

Up to this point, the passage reveals only a little more than we have seen many times before in our reading of *Sons and Lovers*. Once again, we see that marriage, because it is simply something that society expects everyone to enter into at a certain age, is taken far too lightly. Once again, we see that relationships, especially within marriage, are made difficult by the duality, the self-division, within individuals. Clara, like Paul and his mother, is much more radically split within than her husband is, than Miriam or Walter Morel are. Thus, the novel suggests, complex, ambivalent, or self-conflicted selves would be better off with someone like themselves, so that each nature of each individual would have a similar nature to speak and respond to in the other individual. "It was something like your mother and father," Miriam says in response to Paul's assertion that Clara is a complex, two-sided character who was therefore doomed to harbor a "deadened" and "dormant" woman within. By saying so, Miriam implies that Paul's mother, like Clara, was made but "half-alive" by marriage. Surprisingly, Paul does not completely agree, and his failure to concur represents a slight change in the pitch and direction of the novel:

"Yes; but my mother, I believe, got real joy and satisfaction out of my father at first. I believe she had a passion for him; that's why she stayed with him. After all, they were bound to each other."

"Yes," said Miriam.

"That's what one *must have*, I think," he continued—"the real, real flame of feeling through another person—once, only once, if it only lasts three months. See, my mother looks as if she'd *had* everything that was necessary for her living and developing. There's not a tiny bit of feeling of sterility about her."

"No," said Miriam.

"And with my father, at first, I'm sure she had the real thing. She knows; she has been there. You can feel it about her, and about him, and about hundreds of people you meet every day; and, once it has happened to you, you can go on with anything and ripen."

"What happened, exactly?" asked Miriam.

"It's so hard to say, but the something big and intense that changes you when you really come together with somebody else. It almost seems to fertilise your soul and make it that you can go on and mature. . . ."

"And you think Clara never had it?"

"I'm sure."

Miriam pondered this. She saw what he was seeking—a sort

of baptism of fire in passion, it seemed to her. She realised that he would never be satisfied till he had it. (317–18)

By the time we finish the novel, we have reason to doubt Paul's judgment here of the Clara-Baxter relationship, because there is reason to believe that Clara's soul *has* been "fertilised" by her husband. "When I had Baxter, actually had him, then I *did* feel as if I had all of him," she says to Paul, recalling her marriage, and it is not only Lawrence's italicization that suggests that in having Baxter she had something significant, memorable, life-altering (363). Plus, there is reason to believe that there is more to Baxter than ever met the eye during his younger years. In the chapters that follow the above discussion, Paul discovers the complexity of Baxter Dawes and, therefore, the potential for Clara to "come together" with him and be fully alive. Clara discovers the same thing and, as a consequence of the discovery, returns to her husband:

> "Do you want me, Baxter?" she asked.
> His voice was hoarse as he answered:
> "Do you want to come back to me?"
> She made a moaning noise, lifted her arms, and put them round his neck, drawing him to her. He hid his face on her shoulder, holding her clasped.
> "Take me back!" she whispered, ecstatic. "Take me back, take me back!" And she put her fingers through his fine, thin dark hair, as if she were only semi-conscious. (409)

Even if Baxter is not, in his most complex moments, as complicated as his wife is; even if Clara can only "have it" with Baxter in moments of semiconsciousness when the intellectual side of her nature is relatively inactive; she *has* had it—and will have it again—with her husband. Paul is simply jealous—and wrong.

There is, moreover, reason to doubt Paul's confident-seeming, complementary sense that his mother did once have her soul "fertilized" by her relationship with her husband. For one thing, is there any real evidence that her relationship has allowed her to "go on and mature," or that she has "*had* everything that was necessary for her living and developing," or that she has "ripen[ed]" as an individual, or that she "can go on with anything"? Is there, indeed, "not a tiny bit of feeling of sterility about her"? From the beginning of the novel, she has been a "suffocated" woman living in a world she sees as "a dreary place" (5). If she has had a passionate relationship that would allow her to develop vitally, it has been her relationship to Paul. Paul may, at some level, know and feel guilt about this fact, guilt that he can lessen by pretending, to himself and others, that his mother had all she needed with his father.

There is, however, more evidence in *Sons and Lovers* that Paul is either wrong about the saving power of "the real flame of feeling" or wrong about his mother's having fully experienced that "baptism of fire." The evidence is symbolic, in spite of the fact that it is based on the event in Lawrence's personal life that, above all others, was most horribly real to him, namely, his mother's development of a cancerous tumor, her gradual enervation, and her merciful death.

Lawrence takes the fact of his mother's death and transforms it into a symbol of Gertrude Morel's failure fully to experience the kind of relationship that might have made for a fruitful life. He does so by building, throughout the novel, a network of images involving wounds and diseases and by connecting all of them with inadequate love relationships. He suggests early in the book a possible connection between the fits of depression Paul experiences as a child and his destructive relationship with his father (whose pattern of injuring himself in the mines may not be unrelated to the rhythm of rejection he senses at home). Lawrence goes on to picture an unloved and frustrated hunchback, Fanny, who works in a factory producing products that, themselves, suggest injury literally and impotence symbolically. In William and "Gyp" he pairs a "bronchial subject," whose love for her intended is not really love, with a man who dies of pneumonia before marrying a woman for whom, he admits, he feels no love (131, 120). The reader comes to realize that Paul's body is warred upon by his soul owing to the partial nature of Miriam's love for him: "The place where she . . . touch[ed] him ran hot with friction. He was one internecine battle" because of her (173). Baxter Dawes, separated from his wife, contracts typhoid fever. Gertrude's sickness is introduced simultaneously with her expression of disappointment that Arthur has chosen to be "a thing in a red coat" instead of a "man," and she suffers her first painful episode on the day when Paul burns bread because he was "engrossed with Miriam" (181, 211). Twice, then, Lawrence connects Gertrude's illness with her excessive, almost cancerous, love for her boys. As we watch her die slowly, consumed by a tumor that she says has been there "a long time" and unsupported by a man who has been her husband for a long time as well, we can hardly fail to recall her darkly prophetic words to her late son, William. "My boy," she had warned him, "remember you're taking your life in your hands. . . . *Nothing* is as bad as a marriage that's a hopeless failure. Mine was bad enough" (131–32).

The last paragraph of *Sons and Lovers*, which has been interpreted as a hopeful ending by some critics and as a pessimistic one by others, seems to me to be perfectly ambiguous. It seems, in other words, to be as self-divided and self-conflicted as Lawrence's characters are:

> But no, he would not give in. Turning sharply, he walked towards the city's gold phosphorescence. His fists were shut, his mouth set fast. He would not take that direction, to the darkness, to follow [his mother]. He walked towards the faintly humming, glowing town, quickly. (410)

Paul is for the moment rejecting suicide, the death that can easily result from the lovelessness he feels. What he is turning toward, however, seems unlikely to save him. For although the town is golden, it is humming, mechanical, as well.

We should not be surprised, though, by our sense that the glowing town will not, ultimately, assure Paul's survival and spiritual health, given all that Lawrence has had to say about society's role in complicating the modern disease of division and self-division. We should remember, too, that the novel's ending must be read in light of

Lawrence's belief that it is only through private, not public—passionate, not political—relationships that individuals can be made whole again. Paul, obviously, has not yet found the woman with whom he can experience the "fire baptism" that will renovate himself and his world. Whether he ever will is open to conjecture, since he never appears again in Lawrence's fiction.

He is, however, an autobiographical character, and Lawrence, when he set to work on his final revision of *Sons and Lovers*, had just found the kind of love relationship that Paul is still searching for at the end of the novel. The year after publishing *Sons and Lovers*, Lawrence married Frieda von Richthofen.

Although Paul does not reappear in any of the later works, characters who are what Paul might have grown up to become do, like their author, find saving relationships. One of those is Rupert Birkin, the protagonist (and authorial figure) in *Women in Love*. Another is Will Brangwen, who finds for a while with his wife, Anna, that wholeness of love that is neither purely sexual nor purely spiritual. The following passage is taken from the chapter of *The Rainbow* (1915) in which the Brangwens' honeymoon is described:

> He surveyed the rind of the world: houses, factories, trams, the discarded rind; people scurrying about, work going on, all on the discarded surface. An earthquake had burst it all . . . into unreality, leaving here exposed the inside, the reality: one's own being . . . suddenly become present, revealed . . . with the woman one loved. It was confounding. Things are not what they seem! When he was a child, he had thought a woman was a woman merely by virtue of her skirts and petticoats. And now, lo, the whole world could be divested of its garment, the garment could lie there shed away intact, and one could stand in a new world, a new earth, naked in a new, naked universe.[57]

Will is to learn, of course, that there are inevitably moments of dissatisfaction with the beloved, moments of necessary and even healthy retreat from the beloved—into the self or, alternately, toward the town. Lawrence makes it clear, though, that the best work done in civilization is done by those who have been energized, healed, baptized, transformed by the intense kind of relationship that has eluded—but for a fleeting moment or week or unredemptive year—all the characters in *Sons and Lovers*. Clara and Baxter may have enjoyed such communion, but will they again? Gertrude and Walter may have experienced it, too, but not for long enough to be saved by it. As for Paul: finding, nourishing, and growing with such a relationship is his challenge, his only imaginable—his only possible—future.

NOTES

1. "Nottingham and the Mining Countryside," in *Phoenix: The Post-humous Papers of D. H. Lawrence*, ed. Edward D. McDonald (New York: Viking Press, 1936), 133.

2. Ibid., 134-35.

3. *Sons and Lovers* (New York: Penguin Books, 1983), 1. See the Note on the Text that precedes chapter 1 for the publication history of this readily available version of Lawrence's novel. All future citations of the novel refer to this edition and are made in parentheses within the text.

4. "Nottingham and the Mining Countryside," 134.

5. Frank Kermode, *D. H. Lawrence* (New York: Viking Press, 1973), 5.

6. Ibid., 86.

7. "Nottingham and the Mining Countryside," 139.

8. *Study of Thomas Hardy*, in *Phoenix*, ed. McDonald, 481.

9. *The Letters of D. H. Lawrence*, ed. James T. Boulton, 8 vols. (Cambridge: Cambridge University Press, 1979–), 1:476–77.

10. Graham Hough, *The Dark Sun: A Study of D. H. Lawrence* (New York: Macmillan Co., 1957), 40.

11. Ibid., 39, 36.

12. Julian Moynahan, *The Deed of Life: The Novels and Tales of D. H. Lawrence* (Princeton, N.J.: Princeton University Press, 1963), 20.

13. Peter Scheckner, *Class, Politics, and the Individual: A Study of the Major Works of D. H. Lawrence* (London and Toronto: Farleigh Dickinson University Press, 1985), 26.

14. *The Letters of D. H. Lawrence*, 1:476.

15. Harold Massingham, review in the *Daily Chronicle*, 17 June 1913; reprint, in *D. H. Lawrence: The Critical Heritage*, ed R. P. Draper (New York: Barnes & Noble, 1970), 63.

16. Anonymous review in the *Westminster Gazette*, 14 June 1913; reprint, in *Critical Heritage*, 60.

17. Anonymous review in the *Saturday Review*, 21 June 1913; reprint, in *Critical Heritage*, 66.

18. Alfred Kuttner, review in the *New Republic*, 10 April 1915; reprint, in *Critical Heritage*, 79.

19. Ibid., 80.

20. Louise Maunsell Field, review in the *New York Times Book Review*, 21 September 1913; reprint, in *Critical Heritage*, 75.

21. Anonymous review in the *Saturday Review*, 21 June 1913; reprint, in *Critical Heritage*, 65.

22. Anonymous review in the *Standard*, 30 May 1913; reprint, in *Critical Heritage*, 58.

23. Harold Massingham, review in the *Daily Chronicle*, 17 June 1913; reprint, in *Critical Heritage*, 62.

24. Lascelles Abercrombie, review in the *Manchester Guardian*, 2 July 1913; reprint, in *Critical Heritage*, 67–68.

25. Ibid., 67.

26. E. T. [Jessie (Chambers) Wood], *D. H. Lawrence: A Personal Record* (London: Jonathan Cape, 1935).

27. Richard Aldington, *D. H. Lawrence: Portrait of a Genius But ...* (London: Heinemann, 1950; New York: Duell, Sloan & Pearce, 1950), 22, 115.

28. Ibid., 52.

29. Ibid., 148.

30. F. R. Leavis, *D. H. Lawrence: Novelist* (New York: Alfred A. Knopf, 1955), 5–7.

31. Ibid., 178.

32. Hough, *The Dark Sun*, 36, 38–39.

33. Ibid., 49.

34. Ibid., 36.

35. Ibid., 42–43.

36. Mark Schorer, "Technique as Discovery," *Hudson Review* 1, no. 1 (Spring 1948); partial reprint, in *D. H. Lawrence and "Sons and Lovers": Sources and Criticism*, ed. E. W. Tedlock, Jr. (New York: New York University Press, 1965), 167–68.

37. Schorer, "Technique as Discovery," in *"Sons and Lovers,"* ed. Tedlock, 168.

38. Ibid., 168, 167.

39. Ibid., 166.

Notes

40. Mark Spilka, *The Love Ethic of D. H. Lawrence* (Bloomington: Indiana University Press, 1957), 60, 66, 72.

41. Ibid., 76, 79, 82.

42. Moynahan, *Deed of Life*, 18, 25.

43. Ibid., 14, 18.

44. Ibid., 14–15.

45. H. M. Daleski, *The Forked Flame: A Study of D. H. Lawrence* (Evanston, Ill.: Northwestern University Press, 1965), 44.

46. Ibid., 47.

47. Keith Sagar, *The Art of D. H. Lawrence* (Cambridge: Cambridge University Press, 1966), 19–20.

48. Ibid., 23.

49. Scott Sanders, *D. H. Lawrence: The World of the Five Major Novels* (New York: Viking Press, 1973), 23.

50. Ibid., 28, 35–36.

51. Scheckner, *Class, Politics, and the Individual*, 26, 36–37.

52. Ibid., 28–29.

53. Judith Ruderman, *D. H. Lawrence and the Devouring Mother* (Durham, N.C.: Duke University Press, 1984).

54. *The Complete Poems of D. H. Lawrence*, ed. Vivian de Sola Pinto and Warren Roberts (New York: Viking Press, 1964), 36.

55. Ibid., 62.

56. "Poetry of the Present," Introduction to the American edition of *New Poems* (New York: B. W. Huebsch, 1920); reprint, in *The Complete Poems*, 182–83.

57. *The Rainbow* (New York: Random House, 1943), 140.

BIBLIOGRAPHY

Primary Sources

Sons and Lovers. London: Duckworth & Son, 1913. The novel was published in New York by Mitchell Kennerly in the same year; it was republished by the Viking Press in 1933 and consequently reprinted, in Great Britain and the United States, in various Viking, Viking Compass, Viking Penguin, and Penguin editions.

The Letters of D. H. Lawrence. 8 vols. Edited by James T. Boulton. Cambridge: Cambridge University Press, 1979–. At the time this study went to press, three of the projected eight volumes of letters had been published. Volume 1 covers the period 1901–13, volume 2 contains letters written between 1913 and 1916, and volume 3 continues on into June of 1921. The *Letters* form part of the new *Cambridge Edition of the Letters and Works of D. H. Lawrence*.

The Collected Letters of D. H. Lawrence. 2 vols. Edited by Harry T. Moore. London: Heinemann, 1962. Until all eight volumes of the new Cambridge edition of *The Letters of D. H. Lawrence* have been published, readers will need to consult, on occasion, this fine but incomplete collection.

"Nottingham and the Mining Countryside." In *Phoenix: The Posthumous Papers of D. H. Lawrence*, edited by Edward D. McDonald. New York: Viking Press, 1936.

Secondary Sources

Bibliographies

McDonald, Edward D. *A Bibliography of the Writings of D. H. Lawrence.* Philadelphia: Centaur Bookshop, 1925. Books and periodicals. Also contains a list of early studies and reviews of Lawrence.

———. *The Writings of D. H. Lawrence, 1925–1930: A Bibliographical Supplement.* Philadelphia: Centaur Bookshop, 1931. Books and periodicals that appeared after the volume cited above was published.

Roberts, Warren. *A Bibliography of D. H. Lawrence.* London: Rupert Hart-Davis, 1963. The standard bibliography of Lawrence. More complete than the early bibliographies by McDonald.

Sagar, Keith. *The Art of D. H. Lawrence.* See listing below.

Biography and Memoirs

Aldington, Richard. *D. H. Lawrence: Portrait of a Genius But . . .* London: Heinemann, 1950; New York: Duell, Sloan & Pearce, 1950. An early critical biography that is, at the same time, a revised, memorial biography. Aldington reads *Sons and Lovers* almost as if it were straight autobiography. The title of this study indicates something about attitudes contained therein.

Delavenay, Emile. *D. H. Lawrence: The Man and His Work: The Formative Years, 1885–1919.* Translated by K. M. Delavenay. Carbondale: Southern Illinois University Press, 1972. Originally published in French in 1969. A great deal of research has gone into this project, and many interesting facts about the young D. H. Lawrence emerge. The author, however, seems in places to have misunderstood Lawrence's English.

E. T. [Jessie (Chambers) Wood]. *D. H. Lawrence: A Personal Record.* London: Jonathan Cape, 1935. This book, written by the "Miriam" of *Sons and Lovers,* tells of the author's relationship to Lawrence, of the books the two read together, of the autobiographical dimensions of *Sons and Lovers.* For Wood, however, there are no other dimensions; indeed, she seems to have interpreted *Sons and Lovers* as a direct personal attack, and to have written *D. H. Lawrence: A Personal Record* in order to defend herself against a cruel and ungrateful—and inaccurate—former friend.

Lawrence, Frieda. *Not I, But the Wind.* New York: Viking Press, 1934. A well-written, intriguing account of Lawrence written by his flamboyant, intelligent wife. Frieda met Lawrence in 1912, the year before *Sons and*

Lovers was published, so her biography picks up more or less at the point at which Lawrence's semiautobiographical novel leaves off. Still, this book will prove rewarding to anyone who has developed an interest in Lawrence's life and art.

Moore, Harry T. *The Priest of Love: A Life of D. H. Lawrence* Rev. ed. Carbondale: Southern Illinois University Press, 1974. A revised edition of *The Priest of Love* as printed by Farrar, Straus & Giroux, which was first published as *The Intelligent Heart: The Story of D. H. Lawrence* (New York: Farrar, Straus, & Cudahy, 1954). This retitled and revised biography of Lawrence is straightforward, sensible, and easy to read. When it appeared in 1954, Moore's largely sympathetic portrayal of Lawrence contained new material on Lawrence's youth. The text is somewhat achronological, sometimes jarringly so. The photographs are fascinating.

Nehls, Edward, ed. *D. H. Lawrence: A Composite Biography.* 3 vols. Madison: University of Wisconsin Press, 1957–59. This is as much a "primary" source as it is a secondary one, and it is, essentially, implied biography, for what Nehls has done is to ingeniously stitch together innumerable letters and other written fragments in such a way that they tell the story of Lawrence's life.

Literary Criticism

Daleski, H. M. *The Forked Flame: A Study of D. H. Lawrence.* Evanston, Ill.: Northwestern University Press, 1965. A study of Lawrence's dualism, of his view that consciousness contains a "dark" and a "light" side, a "tiger" and a "lamb." This theory leads to the contention that Lawrence at once damns and praises characters like Walter Morel, for the author, like his characters, is divided within.

Draper, Ronald P. *D. H. Lawrence.* New York: Twayne Publishers, 1964. In the Twayne English Authors series, this book begins with an overview of Lawrence's life and thought, and proceeds by surveying the early novels (including *Sons and Lovers*), the major novels, the "pseudo-novels," the late novels, the tales, and the poems. Although necessarily brief, Draper's discussion of *Sons and Lovers* provides a good general account of the work. It is seen, first, as a working-class novel; second, as a novel about maternal love and its relationship to sexual love.

———, ed. *D. H. Lawrence: The Critical Heritage.* New York: Barnes & Noble, 1970. An anthology of early reviews of all the volumes of fiction, nonfiction, and poetry published by Lawrence during his lifetime. Ends with nine obituaries.

Hough, Graham. *The Dark Sun: A Study of D. H. Lawrence.* New York: Macmillan Co., 1957. A well-balanced critical study of "The Major

Bibliography

Novels," "The Tales," "The Poems," and "The Doctrine" of D. H. Lawrence. Hough calls *Sons and Lovers* "the first Freudian novel in English" and believes it to be a flawed, autobiographical work in which Lawrence solved nagging personal problems. Lawrence's doctrine, as interpreted by Hough, is dualistic, naturalistic, and pantheistic. God resides in nature without and the blood within as self-healing sexual mystery.

Kermode, Frank. *D. H. Lawrence.* New York: Viking Press, 1973. A helpful introduction to Lawrence's entire career, this brief critical biography in the Viking Modern Masters series divides the canon up into works produced during four distinct periods: 1913–17, 1917–21, 1922–25, 1925–30. Because Kermode covers eighteen works in 160 pages, there is no time for critical analysis. The book is helpful, however, in seeing Lawrence in light of contemporary intellectual, political, and aesthetic movements.

Leavis, F. R. *D. H. Lawrence: Novelist.* New York: Alfred A. Knopf, 1955. A landmark reading of the "major" novels and tales by one of the great British critics of the century. Leavis was largely responsible for convincing Anglo-American critics of Lawrence's importance, of his place in the "great tradition" of the English novel. Leavis does not believe *Sons and Lovers* to be "major" or "great"; he concentrates on *The Rainbow* and *Women in Love.*

Moynahan, Julian. *The Deed of Life: The Novels and Tales of D. H. Lawrence.* Princeton, N.J.: Princeton University Press, 1963. Moynahan, who views *Sons and Lovers* as "a sort of neurotic case history," argues that a belief in "vitalism" pervades Lawrence's fiction. Characters are saved who live passionately; other forms of living are really forms of decay, dissolution, death. Lawrence's "art" lies in his ability to construct a narrative form through which vitalist narrative and characters interlock and compete with more conventional points of view and characters.

Niven, Alistair. *D. H. Lawrence: The Writer and His Work.* London: Longman, 1980. A volume in the Writers and their Work series published by Longman, this brief book treats Lawrence's life, ten novels, the poetry, and other writings, all in a little over a hundred pages. Nonetheless, the opening chapter (entitled "The Writer and the Man") and the ten pages devoted to *Sons and Lovers* offer valuable, if basic, insights to the undergraduate student reading Lawrence for the first time.

Ruderman, Judith. *D. H. Lawrence and the Devouring Mother.* Durham, N.C.: Duke University Press, 1984. Ruderman argues that the chauvinistic, so-called "leadership novels" of Lawrence's late, political phase are not so distinct from the early novels about families and male-female relationships as critics have heretofore believed. She grounds Lawrence's ideas about male leadership in the fear of dependency on nurturing women, which she in turn traces back to the child's simultaneous desire to return to the womb and fear of suffocation, annihilation, by the mother.

Sagar, Keith. *The Art of D. H. Lawrence*. Cambridge: Cambridge University Press, 1966. A reading of major works in chronological order. Each of the eleven chapters is devoted to a period. Each begins with a brief biographical sketch, continues by providing a bibliography of all works published, and ends with an analytical discussion of one or two texts. Sagar looks for the inner coherence in each and elucidates distinctive themes. Then he locates the work vis à vis contemporary minor works and earlier and later major ones. The chapter on *Sons and Lovers* is entitled "The Bases of the Normal."

Sanders, Scott. *D. H. Lawrence: The World of the Five Major Novels*. New York: Viking Press, 1973. Sanders discusses *Sons and Lovers, The Rainbow, Women in Love, The Plumed Serpent,* and *Lady Chatterley's Lover*. He argues that dichotomies in Lawrence's fiction involving body/mind, instinct/idea, workers/managers, artistocracy/democracy, paganism/Christianity, black/white races, and silence/language may all be related to a more fundamental dichotomy between nature and culture.

Scheckner, Peter. *Class, Politics, and the Individual: A Study of the Major Works of D. H. Lawrence*. London and Toronto: Farleigh Dickinson University Press, 1985. The title accurately describes the emphasis. Lawrence's major novels and stories are seen as expressions of distinct phases of the author's developing social consciousness. Scheckner sees *Sons and Lovers, The Rainbow,* and *Women in Love* as novels about the individual's relationship to society. Later chapters are entitled "Class Conflict and Reaction," "Revolution and Retreat," and "Radical Commitment to Eros." This last chapter argues that in *Lady Chatterley's Lover* Lawrence made his last attempt at reconciling the social classes by trying to rekindle a religious sense of their oneness.

Spilka, Mark. *The Love Ethic of D. H. Lawrence*. Bloomington: Indiana University Press, 1957. This book traces Lawrence's "message" that there are destructive—and healing—forms of love and his "ethic," which is a "life-morality," through five major novels, including *Sons and Lovers*. He also concentrates on Lawrence's "religious dimension." Spilka has been accused of sounding more like a disciple than a critic, but he does an excellent job of showing how inextricable are the aesthetic and prophetic sides of Lawrence's temperament and works.

———, ed. *D. H. Lawrence: A Collection of Critical Essays*. Englewood Cliffs, N.J.: Prentice-Hall, 1963. An excellent collection of essays on Lawrence, edited by the author of *The Love Ethic of D. H. Lawrence*. The essay on *Sons and Lovers* is a famous chapter from *The English Novel: Form and Function* by Dorothy Van Ghent. In this reprinted chapter, entitled simply "On Sons and Lovers," Van Ghent argues that although Lawrence does not use conventional narrative form, he writes with a poetic logic and uses extensively developed imagery to convey his sense of the human self and its complex forms.

Bibliography

Tedlock, E. W. Jr., ed. *D. H. Lawrence and "Sons and Lovers": Sources and Criticism*. New York: New York University Press, 1965. A collection of letters and essays divided into three sections: "Origins" contains letters by Lawrence and one by Alice Dax ("Clara") to Lawrence's wife, plus excerpts from Jessie Chambers's ("Miriam's") *D. H. Lawrence: A Personal Record*. The second section, "Freudian Connections and Approaches," reprints psychoanalytic accounts of the novel written by early reviewers and later critics. The third section, "Technique and Values," contains essays showing how Lawrence uses craftsmanship and form to advance ideas. A portion of Mark Schorer's "Technique as Discovery," originally printed in the first number of the *Hudson Review*, is reprinted here.

INDEX

Due to the nature of this book, the following index lists names, works other than *Sons and Lovers,* and subjects other than those developed on nearly every page of the volume: love, sex, conflict, self-division, male, female, sex roles, physicality, intellect, spirituality. Under "Lawrence, David Herbert" I have confined myself to listing facts, names, and ideas listed neither in the "Chronology" nor under general subject headings.

Index

ABOUT THE AUTHOR

Ross C Murfin is professor of English and associate dean of the College of Arts and Sciences at the University of Miami. He has won numerous awards for undergraduate teaching. Together with his wife and two children, he lives on the campus of the University of Miami in the Honors Residential College, which he serves as Master.

From 1974 to 1981, Professor Murfin taught at Yale University, where he was first an assistant, later an associate, professor of English. The author of numerous articles on Victorian and modern literature, Professor Murfin is best known for his two previous books, both of which are devoted to D. H. Lawrence: *Swinburne, Hardy, Lawrence and the Burden of Belief* was published in 1978 by the University of Chicago Press; the University of Nebraska Press published his study *The Poetry of D. H. Lawrence: Texts and Contexts* in 1983. More recently, Professor Murfin has edited and introduced a collection of critical reassessments of Joseph Conrad. Entitled *Conrad Revisited: Essays for the Eighties,* the collection was published by the University of Alabama Press in 1985.

Professor Murfin received his bachelor's degree from Princeton University and his Ph.D. from the University of Virginia.